Peak

The Future of Travel

David Metz

This print edition first published in
February 2014 by Landor LINKS
Apollo House
359 Kennington Lane
London SE11 5QY
Tel: +44 (0) 207 091 7851

ISBN 978-1-899650-74-3

A catalogue record for this book is available from the British Library.

Contents

Introduction

Travel and transport are an important part of our lives. On average, we spend about an hour a day on the move, mostly for the daily journeys that get us to work, the shops, schools and the rest. Decisions about where we live and how we travel are big decisions, as are the decisions made by governments and businesses about investment in new transport facilities. But we don't think as clearly as we might about these decisions, which determine important aspects of our lives in ways we seldom examine. As a result, the transport systems we have are not as good as they could be.

I will argue that many transport professionals are trapped in out-dated modes of thought and are overlooking new trends in travel behaviour. Some past transport investment has been damaging, while beneficial investment opportunities have been neglected, both the result of professional myopia. Huge expenditures on transport infrastructure are planned in Britain based on obsolete analysis of the supposed benefits and overstated forecasts of the demand for travel. We need to recognise that we have come to the end of one era of travel and are starting out on another. Only by understanding this will we be able to improve the mobile world in which we live.

There are very many travel books—books about interesting journeys to unusual destinations by venturesome travellers. There are also a multitude of books about one or other aspect of transport—steam railways, sailing ships, classic cars, horsedrawn vehicles, aviation, how we drive, how to drive. But there are remarkably few books about why and how we travel. To the best of my knowledge, this book is the first for the general reader. My previous book, *The Limits to Travel,* published in 2008, reached only a professional readership.

The title of this book, *Peak Car*, reflects the idea that car use in developed economies has reached a maximum. Car ownership and use has grown steadily over the past century to reach a peak, from which it may be declining, at least in certain locations such as large and growing cities. The evidence to support this contention is emerging, as are some ideas about what is happening in society that has led to this reversal of trend. Cessation of growth of car use is helpful in the context of concerns about carbon emissions and climate change.

The term 'peak car' was popularised by Phil Goodwin, formerly Professor of Transport Policy at the Centre for Transport Studies, University College London, and currently Emeritus Professor. He originally developed the idea in 2010 in a series of articles in his regular column in the estimable magazine, *Local Transport Today*, and subsequently published a journal article and edited a special issue of a journal on the topic.

The peak car idea was relevant to a line of argument that I myself had been developing for some years, based on analysis carried out while a visiting professor at University College London. My interest in travel and transport started when I was appointed as Chief Scientist at the UK Department for Transport, the final civil service post I held during a twenty-year career in a number of government departments. I left the Department feeling dissatisfied with the analytical methods used there to model the consequences and appraise the value of new transport investments. This unsatisfactory approach to analysis led to mistaken investment and policy decisions, it seemed to me.

Since leaving the Department, I have devoted some effort to addressing the deficiencies of the conventional approaches to analysis developed by transport economists and adopted by governments. I have published my analysis and conclusions in a succession of papers in peer-reviewed journals, where pretty rigorous scrutiny ensures the high quality of what gets published, and where ideas that run counter to the prevailing orthodoxy (like mine) get closely inspected. This book summarises my conclusions in a form that I hope is accessible to all those interested in why and how we travel, including transport professionals.

The themes of this book apply to travel worldwide, particularly in the developed countries with high levels of car use, but also to developing countries as car ownership grows. In practice, much of my evidence is taken from experience of travel and transport in Britain, which is where I live and so have the most direct familiarity, both as a participant and an observer. This allows me to see the whole picture, both the main elements and the detailed interactions.

An important reason for the focus on Britain is the extensive data available, mainly through the efforts over many years of the statisticians at the UK Department for Transport and the willingness of the senior management and ministers to support this data collection. While I am critical of aspects of the Department's analysis and policy formulation, I am pleased to be able to compliment it for collecting what are probably the most extensive and comprehensive national travel and transport statistics of any country. Regional and local statistics are generally more limited, although those for London are probably the best for any large city in the world. I pay particular attention to travel and transport in London, not only because that is where I live and have first hand experience, but also because recent developments may point the way to how successful large cities across the globe might prosper in the future by meeting the mobility needs of their growing populations.

While my focus is on Britain, on account of the availability of statistics to underpin the analysis, I draw upon data from other countries to argue that the developed economies are broadly similar as far as travel behaviour is concerned. Perhaps the main difference amongst these countries is the extent of the historic railway system that has been preserved and can be modernised—generally important in Europe, less so elsewhere.

This is a short book, about 35 thousand words, half the length or less of a conventional book. Life is brief and there are too many books to read, so if an argument can be made concisely and cogently, that is worth doing. The ebook format allows wide distribution at a price low enough not to inhibit readers interested in the topic (a print version is also available). But the short length means that a number of important aspects of travel and transport are rather neglected, for instance safety, environmental impacts, disability and gender issues, and health benefits of walking and cycling. These topics were covered in my previous book and the arguments have not changed, nor are my views different from mainstream thinking.

The central argument that I make in this book is that we have come to the end of an era in which we have steadily travelled more, made possible by a succession of innovative transport technologies permitting faster travel. In the new era, we have sufficient choices and opportunities largely to meet our needs. What we now want from the transport system is better quality. I shall explore how we might achieve that outcome.

William Gibson, the science fiction writer who coined the term 'cyberspace', said: 'The future is already here—it's just not evenly distributed.' We know that the future for most countries will feature significant demographic change—larger populations, increasing longevity, more urban living at increasing density. Cities that are already meeting the needs for mobility, access and choice of growing populations allow us to glimpse a future that is already here. Living in London while writing this book has provided a useful vantage point from which to speculate about the global future of travel.

I will be following up this book with a blog on my website, www.davidmetz.org. Comments are welcome.

Chapter One:

Three Eras of Travel

We find ourselves situated in time and space. While the flow of time carries us forward inexorably, we have some choice about where we locate ourselves and how we use the time granted to us. History and geography, the disciplines of time and space, are both possible only because people are mobile and can travel. If humans were rooted like plants, we would have much less to say. Travel is central to our existence, yet too often we take it for granted—at least until we are immobilised, through injury for instance, when the difficulty of getting around brings home quite forcibly the crucial importance of movement.

There have been vast changes to the pattern of human mobility over the past two centuries, which we need to understand if we are to see how this might develop in the future. I will argue that the future of travel will not be like the past in some important aspects, and that we are at a point of transition. But first, we need to go back to the beginning of human history.

Ancestors

Humans are descended from tree-living ancestors who evolved to walk on two legs. Compared with other primates, the human leg is lengthened and the foot narrowed and elongated to facilitate striding. Our ancestors originated in Africa and migrated over the past 60,000 years to all the habitable parts of the world. Over this period people travelled on foot, mostly the daily routine of foraging for food, hunting animals and gathering plants and fruits, but also the occasional longer journeys to find new habitats. Humans are good at running as well as walking. We have evolved an anatomy and physiology that allows expert hunters from the surviving forager societies to outrun deer and antelope. Although these animals can sprint faster, the hunters relentlessly pursue them until the creatures collapse in the noonday heat. Humans are equipped with sweat glands, which these animals lack, and can formulate strategies for a successful pursuit.

There is some evidence of a genetic basis for a tendency to curiosity and restlessness, as found in nomadic lifestyles. More important may be the evolution of legs and hips that permit long distance walking. Certainly, the evolutionary success of modern humans has depended on the propensity to move on to new hunting grounds when prey became depleted. The Neanderthals, our ancestral relatives, did not migrate beyond Europe and adjacent parts of Asia; perhaps for that reason they failed to survive.

Evidence from remaining hunter-gatherer societies indicates that members typically spend on average only three or four hours a day on the move, foraging for food. The rest of their time is devoted to leisure and domestic tasks. This means that individuals on average travel some three or four thousand miles a year. Lifestyles changed following the Neolithic Revolution that started in the Middle East 10,000 years ago, with cultivation of plants and domestication of animals. These farmers worked hard because they could secure increasing returns from their efforts, in contrast to the foragers who were subject to diminishing returns as their wild food sources becomes scarcer and who then had to move on to new territory. This limited their opportunity for owning possessions and for house construction, unlike the settled farmers who could accumulate goods and support the first stonebuilt cities like Jericho.

Once people settled in communities, busy in fields and workshops, the need to travel was much less. Time for travel was at a premium, competing with time for working, eating, sleeping and socialising, all between sunrise and sunset. It seems that individuals spent around an hour a day travelling on average. Evidence comes from modern, low-income rural communities and from the size of historic settlements, where it rarely took more than an hour to walk from the centre to the edge of the territory, whether the land holdings of the village or the boundaries of the city. In an hour a day, at walking speed, the average distance travelled reduced to about a thousand miles a year. Horsedrawn carts and carriages on poor roads made little difference to the average speed of travel, which did not begin to increase until less than two hundred years ago, with the invention of the railway.

Faster Travel

The first public railway opened in 1825 between Stockton and Darlington in northeast Britain, with the first intercity service between Liverpool and Manchester commencing five years later. Over the next twenty years, 7,000 miles of railway were built—a remarkable achievement considering that the rail network in Britain currently totals just 9,000 miles. This construction boom stemmed from people's huge desire to travel beyond the village or town of their birth, and from the willingness of investors to put up money to profit from that desire. Similar enthusiasm for railway construction was displayed in Europe, the Americas, India and elsewhere.

At around the time railway construction was beginning, improvements to roads were also taking place. The Scottish surveyor, John McAdam, developed road construction based on small pieces of broken stone of defined size which provided better running for coaches with narrow, iron-tyred wheels, as well as resisting degradation. Better roads allowed big improvements in the speed of mail coaches, cutting the time from

London to Holyhead (for the ferry to Dublin) from 41 to 28 hours. However, by 1837 the mail on this route was being carried by rail, and for much of the nineteenth century roads were neglected.

Interest in roads revived with the invention of the bicycle, the first recognizably modern type being made in Coventry in 1885. The first motorcycle powered by an internal combustion engine was also produced in 1885, by the German engineer Daimler, who with Otto, Maybach and Benz pioneered use of the petrolfuelled engines for the first motorcars. Benz's wife, Bertha, could claim to be the first motorist when she made a halfday 100 km excursion without her husband's knowledge. The early cars were annoying to the public because of the dust thrown up from the loose road surface once car speeds exceeded 20 mph. The answer was to bind the top layer of stones with bitumen, a naturally occurring oil tar material, or to use as the top layer asphalt, a natural mixture of bitumen and local rock. Subsequently tar from coal gas production or from oil refining was used to bind stone, with the term 'tarmac' used to describe blacktopped road surfaces or airfields.

An important innovation was the pneumatic tyre, introduced by John Dunlop in 1888 specifically for bicycles and made widely available for cars from 1900. These airfilled tyres gave a more comfortable ride, were safer because the contact area with the road surface was greater than for a solid tyre, and for the same reason reduced road surface wear. Pneumatic tyres were essential to achieve speeds in excess of 20 mph.

The succession of improvements—to railways, roads, vehicles and the engines that powered them—in the course of the nineteenth and twentieth centuries allowed faster travel for more and more of the population. This culminated in the widespread ownership of the motorcar, of which there are approaching 30 million on the roads of Britain. Global vehicle production exceeds 80 million annually.

The car has not changed fundamentally since the first massproduced Model T Ford a century ago—an internal combustion engine consuming fuel refined from crude oil, propelling, via a gearbox, four rubbertyred wheels, all controlled by an amateur chauffeur. Despite some 200,000 road casualties a year in Britain, including 1,750 fatalities, we are willing to allow ourselves to take charge of vehicles that can cause death and destruction, because the benefits from mobility are so great.

Over 80 per cent of non-walking trips in Britain are now by car. Like other developed countries, we have come to rely on the car for mobility. The consequence of the development of the railways in the nineteenth century and the car in the twentieth is that over the past two hundred years the average distance travelled on land in Britain by all modes of transport (including walking) has risen from 1,000 to 7,000 miles a year. This has happened as the result of travelling faster in an unchanged amount of time—the hour a day devoted to travel that is found in all settled societies. The number of journeys meanwhile has remained the same at about 1,000 trips a year on average. Moreover, the purpose of our daily journeys has changed little in recent years. The most popular journey purpose is shopping, whether to the corner shop to buy the newspapers, the weekly trip by car to the supermarket or the expedition to a shopping centre for less frequent purchases. After shopping comes, in descending order, visiting friends, commuting to work, travelling to school or college, personal business, and escorting others, together with a variety of purposes that require travelling less than once a week.

Why travel further?

So why do we travel further for the same purposes? The answer: to have more access to places and the increased choice and opportunities that go with this—more choice of jobs that we can get to from where we live, more choice of homes accessible from our work place, more choice of shops, schools and so on. Suppose you live in a village where the bus service is poor or nonexistent and you don't have use of a car. Choices of jobs, schools, shops, leisure activities are all very limited. This was the situation generally in Britain two centuries and more ago and remains the case for many older people and others who can't drive. It also applies to much of the population in the developing economies. Enlarging personal horizons is a powerful motivation to seek more mobility. The cheapest means is the bicycle, once common in Britain before widespread car ownership, now undergoing a revival as a healthy way to travel to work and get around. The motorized two-wheelers, so prevalent in the cities of the developing world, provide additional mobility, particularly in hilly terrain. But the car is what most people desire for speedy personal travel, as well as to carry passengers, shopping and other bulky items, and to protect from the weather. The car is deservedly popular and seems certain to remain so, despite traffic congestion, casualties and vehicle emissions—detriments for which some solutions exist.

Recently, however, something unexpected has emerged. The average daily distance travelled in Britain grew to reach 7,000 miles a year and then stopped increasing around 1995, as shown in Figure 1. This displays data from the National Travel Survey, which has been commissioned by the UK Department for Transport for 40 years, and which covers all modes of travel except international travel by air (discussed in Chapter 4). It is the longest running survey of its kind internationally, has the largest coverage of aspects of travel, and I draw upon it extensively in this book as evidence which I interpret.

Figure 1. Average distance travelled, travel time and trips per person per year in Britain

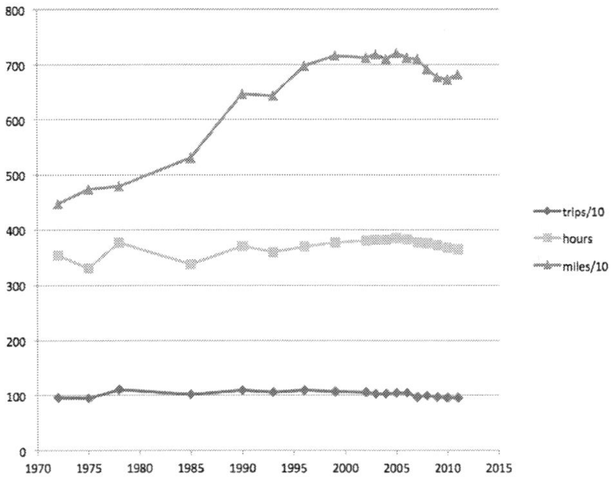

Figure 1 also shows that the average amount of travel time has held steady over the past 40 years at about 370 hours a year, or an hour a day, and the number of journeys has remained close to 1,000 per person per year. So the pattern of daily travel has stabilised. (I use the term 'daily travel' since we are talking mainly about the journeys we make frequently, to work, school, the shops and so forth.) There is a small dip in distance travelled in the most recent years, probably due to the economic downturn.

Car use per person has also stopped growing in Britain, not surprising given the dominance of the car in daily mobility—responsible for almost 80 per cent of the current average distance travelled in Britain. Growth of car use has also halted in other developed economies in recent years, including—

perhaps surprisingly—the United States where vehicle-miles travelled per person ceased to grow after 2000. I will discuss some of the specific reasons for changing car use later. For now, I focus on the question: why has personal travel ceased to grow, following the previous two hundred years of continued increase?

My explanation is that access, opportunities and choice increase with the square of the speed—because what is accessible falls within a circle, the centre of which is where you are now, the radius (r) of which is proportional to the speed of travel, and the area of which is proportional to the radius or speed squared (area of a circle = πr^2, if you can remember your school maths). So access and choice increase rather rapidly as the speed of travel increases. Consider three modes of travel: walking at 3 mph, cycling at 10 mph, and driving at 25 mph. The areas of the circles corresponding to 30 minutes travel are 7, 80 and 500 square miles respectively. This illustrates the many more possibilities available as you speed up.

On the other hand, a characteristic of choice is what the economists call 'diminishing marginal utility'. This means that the more choice of a particular kind of thing you have, the less the value of an extra bit of choice. If you have ten pairs of shoes, buying an additional pair is likely to give less satisfaction on the whole than if you started with only two pairs.

Test this idea. Think how many choices of food store you have within say fifteen or twenty minutes of home. If you usually go by car to a large supermarket, count how many of those you can get to. If you usually walk to a smaller local store, count those. Then ask yourself if it would be worthwhile travelling further to have more choice. If not, you have sufficient choice of food stores and your demand for travel to access these has 'saturated', as the economists say. For people living in urban areas of Britain, 80 per cent of us have a choice of three or more large supermarkets within fifteen minutes drive, and 60 per cent have a choice of four or more—pretty high levels of choice and little need to travel further, so it's not too surprising that daily travel for shopping has ceased to grow.

It's not only food stores and supermarkets that are generally readily accessible to those of us in Britain who either have a car, or who can use frequent public transport or bicycles to get around urban areas. Good levels of choice are also to be found for doctors' surgeries and hospitals, for primary and secondary schools and for further education colleges. Of course, sometimes choice can be a bit theoretical. You may have choice of a number of primary schools for your five-year-old, but the most popular can be oversubscribed, as well as giving preference to brothers and sisters of existing pupils. So in practice, choice can be less than might be supposed simply from travel time from home. One response would be to take your child by car to a more distant 'good school', but the scope for that is likely to be limited since such schools will be popular locally.

There is a distinction to be made between destinations that can readily be replicated to meet demand, such as supermarkets, and those that have some special feature that precludes replication. Most housing is replicable—witness rows of terrace houses and those many estates of rather similar 'executive homes'. But the most sought after properties have particular features—whether historic, such as thatched cottages or stately homes, or geographic, such as waterfront locations or especially desirable neighbourhoods—that cannot easily be replicated and which therefore command premium prices. The distinction between replicable and nonreplicable also applies to schools. Schools generally are built to match the number of children of school age, a basic duty of a local education authority. But a 'good school' has outstanding characteristics that are not readily copied—if they could be they would.

Demand for travel to replicable destinations ceases to grow when good levels of choice are available to a mobile population, as for supermarkets. Demand for travel to non-replicable destinations is also constrained, not because there is sufficient choice, but rather because the availability is limited by price, as for property, or by capacity, as for good schools. Another example of a capacity constraint arises with top-ranking football teams. In the past, people supported their local team that was within walking distance of home. Nowadays, those who prefer to support a Premiership team can generally find one with stadium within driving distance, but the best-performing teams tend to sell all the seats, which limits demand for travel to these matches.

So demand for travel to both replicable and non-replicable destinations may be expected to cease to grow—indeed to saturate—for a society with high levels of mobility. There are, however, certain classes of destination where travel demand saturation is not to be anticipated. New houses built on greenfield sites at the edge of existing towns are always popular, both on account of the pleasant location and because they are priced to sell. The price the builder pays for the previously agricultural land ensures this, while allowing the landowner a substantial gain. Greenfield sites made accessible to centres of employment through new transport developments become prime targets for developers who seek planning consent to erect new housing. Although there is substantial choice of housing generally, new greenfield housing is sought after, which means that travel demand to this class of destination would not be expected to saturate. However, in recent years most new housing has been built not on greenfield sites, but within existing urban areas (to be discussed in Chapter 2), which means that the growth of travel resulting from greenfield housing has been small, and not enough to prevent the flattening of the overall rate of growth of travel demand shown in Figure 1.

A second class of travel that is unlikely to be subject to demand saturation is commuting to specialist and senior jobs. Most people in regions not subject to high levels of unemployment have a reasonable choice of job possibilities without having to travel excessively. The average journey to work in Britain is nine miles and takes half an hour. On the other hand, jobs that have higher status and rewards are likely to attract qualified candidates willing to travel further—travel that is affordable given the higher pay on offer. So travel demand to get to such higher status employment may not saturate, and indeed long distance commuting is likely to grow as rail services are improved. Road improvements also allow people to travel further to reach better jobs. Nevertheless, such commuting takes time and money that only a minority find affordable, so the overall impact on the growth of travel is modest.

Enough travel

The idea that we have enough daily travel to meet our reasonable needs for choice of jobs, shops, doctors, schools and other local services depends on our having the means to be mobile. The car meets this need, which is why it is so popular. Good frequent public transport in towns and cities can also meet our needs, and bicycles too for those who are confident to ride them. But there are many who lack such mobility: older people in rural areas never or no longer able to drive; others with disabilities who are unable to drive; and people of all ages not able to afford a car who live away from good public transport. All these risk being socially excluded in our mobile society. Current drivers may expect to grow old and have to give up car use as the result, typically, of onset of a number of minor disabilities—of vision, hearing, cognitive function or lack of dexterity. So it is all our interests, anticipating the needs of our future selves, to support transport facilities that offer good mobility other than by means of the car.

A further feature of the modern transport scene is that it's hard to go faster. Accidents are both more likely and more severe at higher speeds, hence the increasing tendency in Britain to reduce speed limits on urban roads. Energy requirements grow rapidly as speeds increase, to overcome air and other frictional resistance, and carbon emissions increase accordingly. There is some scope for faster rail travel but new high speed rail routes will represent only a small proportion of total travel.

These technical limits to higher travel speeds, which I discuss in more depth in Chapter 5, are a further constraint on the growth of demand for travel, given that the time available for travelling has to be found within the confines of the 24-hour day. It is fortunate that the occurrence of this speed constraint coincides with the point at which we have enough access and choice to meet most of our needs. For both these reasons, the growth of daily travel has reached a plateau.

We've reached the end of an era in human history: the end of the third era of travel. The first era was man as hunter-gatherer, covering around three to four thousand miles a year on foot, and populating the whole of the habitable earth over some 60,000 years. The second era began when people settled in agricultural communities, when work limited travel to about an hour a day on average, allowing one thousand miles or so of travel over a year. The third era started almost two hundred years ago, when harnessing the energy of fossil fuels allowed us to travel increasingly faster and so farther in the hour a day of travel time. Average distance travel in Britain by surface transport steadily increased to about 7,000 miles a year. But growth has now halted. A natural limit to travel has been reached. The third era has now ended, not just in Britain but also in the developed economies generally. We are entering the fourth era of travel. This book is concerned with what it will feel like to be a traveller in this new era.

The study of history allows us to look back to our origins and ancestors. To think about the future, we need to consider our present geography—how we situate ourselves in space and how we move between our locations. This is the subject of the next three chapters.

Chapter Two:

City Living

The way in which society has developed over the last two centuries has led to big changes in where we live. Most people now reside in towns and cities. Two hundred years ago our ancestors predominantly lived in villages and the countryside. This population shift from rural to urban living is unlikely to have had much effect on the amount of time people spent travelling, given all the other daily activities that had to be fitted in. The purposes of our journeys has changed a bit, for instance more journeys to school and fewer to work for young people as education became compulsory and the school leaving age rose. The big change, however, has been in how we travelled.

Think back two centuries to the year 1800 when, if you started from St Paul's Cathedral in the City of London, you could walk for half an hour in most directions and reach the countryside. At its greatest, the builtup area was five miles across, east to west. Nearly all daily travel was on foot, and horsedrawn carriages on poor roads were not much quicker. Opportunities for work were limited by the number of employers within walking distance of where you lived. Choice of homes was limited by the need to be able to get to your place of work in reasonable time, and in the same way other choices were restricted—of shops, schools and other regularly used facilities. But with the first railways in the 1830s, all this began to change. The railway permitted faster travel, which increased the opportunities available. Cheap tickets on early morning trains allowed workers to move out of the urban slums while continuing to be employed in the city centre. The middle classes travelled in from their suburban villas on the later trains, and towns and cities expanded.

Establishing patterns

The pattern of human urban living has been shaped by the introduction of a range of new transport services that arose from the development of innovative transport technologies. Two hundred years ago, only well off urban dwellers could afford to live more than three or four miles from the city centre, using horsedrawn carriages to get around. As incomes grew generally, the inhabitants of towns and cities were able to take advantage of a series of innovations that allowed faster travel and hence more access than is possible on foot. Horsedrawn buses were introduced in London in 1828, carrying 22 passengers on improved roads in the inner suburbs, although the fares limited patronage to the middle classes. Horse trams arrived in 1870; steel wheels on steel rails reduced rolling resistance so that two horses were able to pull 50 passengers, and the working class could afford the lower fares. The first underground trains in London were introduced 150 years ago in 1863, and the motorcar in the 1880s. The modern bicycle became widely used in the 1890s, as did the motorbike. Electric trams arrived in the same decade, and motorbuses in 1915. These new transport services allowed the city to spread and the population to grow. Further development of railways, trams and trunk roads allowed expansion of London in the inter-war years, so that the builtup area became five times what it had been at the beginning of the twentieth century.

For each successive development of transport technology, there has been a corresponding kind of city. However, the previous growth of the city generally shaped and constrained the subsequent transport options. Only rarely was a city restructured, as when Baron Haussmann imposed a network of large avenues on the medieval city structure of Paris in the latter part of the nineteenth century. A contemporary example is the major rebuilding of Beijing underway, with six ring roads and many broad boulevards—and a major problem of traffic congestion.

Average travel time remained broadly constant through this evolution of urban transport systems and has been a contributing factor to the shaping of cities. The successive innovations in transport technology that permitted higher speeds allowed people to travel greater distances in the time available, and lower population densities ensued.

'Walking cities' were the major urban form for eight thousand years and substantial parts of the central areas of many major cities retain this character—dense mixed-use areas no more than 5 km across. 'Public transport ('Transit' in the US) cities' developed from 1850 to 1950 based on trams and trains, allowing spreading from dense centres 2030 km along rail corridors. 'Automobile cities' from the 1950s onwards could spread further at low density to 5080 km.

Cities are characterised by their density and their history. Decisions about future development are 'path-dependent'—they depend on the route previously taken. A relatively recent city like Los Angeles, with low density and high car dependency, is very different from the high densities found in Manhattan or Central London where road capacity for the car is limited and much more use is made of public transport. Fifty years ago, when car ownership was low but growing rapidly, it was thought that cities might be adapted to absorb the car. Many US cities went a long way in that direction, as did some Japanese cities, and as are some Chinese cities, with elevated urban freeways and multi-story parking. A number of British cities damaged their urban fabrics and, arguably, hindered their economic development by trying too hard to accommodate the car.

Winston Churchill said: 'We shape our buildings, and afterwards our buildings shape us.' The same is true of cities. The more attractive and successful cities are those that have pushed back the car in favour of creating space for pedestrians, improving public transport and providing for cycling. The sharing of space between vehicles and pedestrians by removing kerbs and road markings, as advocated by the Dutch traffic engineer Hans Moderman, turns out to enhance both the experience of those on foot as well as traffic efficiency and safety. In European cities, shared space is the result of a specific intervention, as with Exhibition Road in London's museum district. In Asian cities, the sharing of road space is simply natural behaviour—it seems undisciplined but it works.

Canary Wharf in the former Docklands is London's new financial district with headquarters offices for many of the big banks. There are only 3,000 parking spaces for 100,000 staff who therefore commute on public transport, largely the new rail routes. The pioneering Docklands Light Railway showed how accessible was this new district to the City, the original financial centre. Growing demand for travel to Canary Wharf has been met by the extension of the underground Jubilee Line with its grand stations, the refurbished Overground, using the tracks of obsolete rail routes, and soon to come is Crossrail, the new east-west route being tunnelled under central London. Speedy and reliable travel by rail means that this form of public transport is acceptable to the well-paid employees, despite sardine-like packing at peak usage. Road traffic in this new quarter is quite light.

Growing cities

People are migrating to cities because this is where the action is. Currently, 50 per cent of the global population lives in urban areas, projected to increase to 70 per cent by mid-century as rural inhabitants seek to improve themselves and as improving agricultural productivity provides a better living for those who remain. Cities have a choice: they can house their expanding population in new low density suburbs on greenfield sites, where car use is attractive, or in higher density more central areas, often built on former used sites ('brownfield'), where car use is constrained by road space and public transport is more effective. At one time it looked as though the predominant choicc would be suburban or 'exurban', with US 'edge cities' growing just outside existing city limits to provide office space and new homes in proximity, leaving the old commercial centres to die. Recently, however, there has been a revival of city centre activity, with both business services and residences being newly built or converted from historic commercial properties.

London is a leading example of inner city regeneration, both in the Docklands and the neighbourhoods just north of the financial 'square mile' of the old City, Clerkenwell and Shoreditch in particular. At the beginning of the nineteenth century the population of London was one million. It grew to over six million by the beginning of the twentieth century, reaching a peak of over eight million by mid-century. There was then a period of decline, with a loss of 1.2 million during the 1960s and 1970s, as many people chose suburban and rural lifestyles, to take advantage of growing car ownership. After a period of stability in the 1980s, London's population began to grow steadily, from a low of 6.8 million to reach 8.2 million by 2011. The forward projection is for continued growth, with a population of 10 million before 2040. Population growth has occurred within the existing urban boundaries, such that 96 per cent of new housing is on formerly used sites.

Car ownership and use was of course quite low in the middle of the last century, both nationally and in London. Around five per cent of all journeys in London around 1950 were made by car. This proportion steadily rose as prosperity increased and people could afford cars, to reach a peak in the early 1990s when 50 per cent of all journeys were by car. Since then, little new road capacity has been created, which has limited further car use even as the population has grown. In fact, bus and cycle lanes and pedestrian areas have reduced space for cars; parking controls in both in the inner suburbs and central area constrain car use since you can't drive unless you're sure of somewhere to park at the end—which makes supermarkets with parking attractive for the weekly shop; and in central London a pioneering congestion charging zone levies a fixed fee for entry during working hours.

So despite increasing numbers of people and rising incomes, the net result is that number of car trips in London has held steady at about ten million a day over the past twenty years. And because the population has increased, this means that the proportion or share of all trips that are by car has declined from 50 per cent in the early 1990s to 38 per cent in 2011. I project a further decline to around 30 per cent by 2040, given expected continued population growth. In short, we reached a peak in the *share* of journeys in London by car around 1990—the clearest manifestation of the phenomenon known as 'peak car'. The actual number of such journeys reached a plateau ('plateau car', as it might be described).

Public transport use in London has increased to meet the growing needs of those not owning or using cars. Greater demand for public transport means more frequent services with reduced waiting time, which in turn encourages further use. Walking has stayed level over the past twenty years, while cycling is growing, but from a low base.

Similar situations are found in Birmingham and Manchester, the second and third largest British cities, where there is evidence for a peak followed by decline in actual car numbers entering the two city centres during the morning travel to work period. As car numbers have declined, rail passenger numbers have grown in these cities, with bus use fairly steady. Beyond

Britain, declining per capita car use has been reported for a number of Australian, European and American cities in recent years.

Reversing the trend

This relative decline in car use seen in London and other cities is remarkable. Historically and globally, as people have become better off, car ownership and use have increased. But now in London and elsewhere, this trend has reversed. Despite the prosperity of London, car ownership and driving licence holding are well below the national level and still declining. There is little pushback from the public to this steady shift away from car use, and new apartments sell readily in inner boroughs with no offstreet parking nor entitlement to onstreet parking.

These are indications that the love affair with the car may be approaching its end. The car manufacturers are concerned that younger people aspire more to having mobile phones, iPads, and other digital devices, as a reflection of personal style. The proportion of men in their twenties in Britain and other developed countries holding driving licences is in decline, reflecting the cost of car ownership and of learning to drive, but also lifestyle shifts, including the growing numbers in higher education.

Going to a university located in the centre of a city; enjoying a life which does not depend on the car; staying around for the first job or perhaps moving to another city centre; postponing learning to drive because the need is not pressing, insurance expensive and parking space hard to find; being frugal with money on account of student loan repayments; using a bike or walking for exercise and convenience, and public transport for the bigger distances; finding cheap rail fares through student discounts and online advance booking, bus arrival times via apps and delays from twitter feeds; wanting not to worry about drinkdriving on a Friday night; taking pride in software skills, rather than car mechanics; perhaps even preferring video games such as *Grand Theft Auto* ('drive somewhere, shoot something, drive back') to real-life driving—all of these factors seem increasingly common in many developed countries and contribute to the decline in driving amongst younger people.

There is growing recognition of the economic and cultural importance of cities, even in a world in which digital technologies allow us to be dispersed geographically yet interact continuously. It is in cities that we attain critical mass. Persuasive arguments, both economic and cultural, in favour of cities are articulated by two prominent US academics. Richard Florida maintains that metropolitan regions with high concentrations of technology workers, artists and musicians exhibit a higher level of economic development. This well educated 'creative class' fosters an environment that attracts more creative people and the businesses where they work. Edward Glaeser emphasises 'agglomeration economics', which refers to increases in productivity associated with urban proximity: larger pools of skilled staff to draw upon, suppliers and customers close to hand, and spillovers of technical know-how so that ideas diffuse rapidly—both through organised discussion amongst those with similar expertise and in gossip. Agglomeration is why people choose to live in cities—things work better there. Cities reduce the space between people—less space and more people mean greater opportunities for productive interaction.

London is an example of a dynamic world city, with an innovative, English language, service sector attracting both creative entrepreneurs and young people seeking employment in growth businesses such as fashion, retailing, tourism, finance, digital, media, culture, consultancy, law, research and higher education. The trick is to provide rail-based, reliable, swift public transport that can get the professionals out of their cars for work-related journeys. Traffic congestion is then manageable. Otherwise cities jam up with cars since the business classes are reluctant to join the school children, older and poorer travellers on the slower, less reliable buses. Current badly congested cities include Moscow, Delhi, São Paulo, Mexico City, Beijing, Nairobi, Johannesburg and Madrid. The strong desire for car ownership in Moscow led to rapid growth and the first post-Soviet fortune was made not from raw materials but from selling cars. The City's mayor thinks that public transport is for losers and is willing to fund road construction, eliminate traffic signals, and eschew parking controls—with the result that congestion prevails, exacerbated by pushy drivers and emergency-vehicle privileges for the elite.

Successful cities

A successful world city has a growing population—success attracts migrants— and a declining share of journeys being made by car. A successful city needs also to build upwards rather than outwards, to achieve the population density needed for an economically viable public transport system. The Shard in London is the tallest building in the European Union but has only 48 parking spaces. It is centrally located and will rely on public transport for access.

Public transport use varies quite widely between countries, with demand high in Europe compared with the US due to higher density cities, higher taxes on fuel, more expensive parking and fewer parking spaces. Cheap fuel and land permitted growth of low-density cities, particularly in the US, in which the car predominates. Within Europe there are surprisingly large variations in public transport use, with twice as many such trips per person in Switzerland than in the UK (twice as many in Zurich compared with London). The Netherlands has half the number of Britain on account of extensive cycle use. European experience shows that public transport can compete well with the private car in cities, even amongst affluent households, when services are frequent and integrated across the network, ticketing convenient, fares attractive, and where population densities are reasonably high and car use constrained.

London is increasingly following such integrated and complementary policies. This is possible because a single public body is responsible for organising the transport system—Transport for London, which reports to the Mayor. Outside London, the bus services are organised differently, with private companies competing to provide services. The benefits of such on-the-road competition are pretty limited, with bus use in most English cities tending to decline, in contrast to continuing growth in London. These cities also lack a well-developed rail-based public transport system compared with London and so are more dependent on the car. Arguably, this has detracted from the economic success associated with agglomeration.

Demand for rail travel into and between cities has been buoyant in Britain, doubling since a low point in the mid-1990s. Historically, the rail system developed substantially to serve London, both for commuters and for longer distance trips. This London focus now turns out to be very suitable for a world city with declining car ownership and use. Recent and planned investments include the first High Speed Rail link to Europe (known as HS1) and the proposed HS2 to the Midlands and the North.

There is vocal debate about the value of the considerable expenditure that will be required to build HS2. The main issues are the likely economic benefits for the provincial cities that will have speedier links to the capital, and whether the funds could be better employed in improving transport within and between these cities, as a means to stimulate the local economies. My own view is that the best argument for constructing

HS2 is to meet the needs of a growing population of London for travel northwards, a population that is making less use of cars, that owns fewer cars, and therefore which naturally turns increasingly to rail.

This chapter has focused on living in cities in which people are making less use of the car. What is not yet clear is whether the choice of urban lifestyles by younger people reflects a long-term preference for the buzz of the city, or just a postponement of an eventual move to the suburbs. It is to the suburbs I now turn.

Chapter Three:

Suburban Societies

Towns and cities have grown larger as improved transport has allowed their inhabitants to travel to the centre while living in more spacious and pleasant neighbourhoods. Inner and outer suburbs developed over the past two centuries where cities had adjacent land suitable for housing. The middle classes abandoned many of the more central residential areas of Britain's Georgian and early Victorian cities as coal burn contributed to the peasouper fogs and general grime. But once legislation to prohibit dirty coal use was enacted in 1956, in response to London's Great Smog of 1952, and once natural gas was adopted generally for heating, these inner suburbs were recovered and 'gentrified' by those of the middle classes who preferred the convenience of location close to all the city centre has to offer.

But the greater part of the urban population now lives in outer suburbs built mainly in the twentieth century. Feelings about these outer suburbs are mixed. For most people, they are pleasant places in which to raise families and then to continue to live in the empty nest when children have left home, near to old friends and neighbours, gardens to be tended, social activities and shops accessible easily by car, with parking usually possible. For some, however, the suburbs are a second-best sprawl of socially segregated, low density, standardised housing, necessitating car-dependence, with traffic levels that discourage children from roaming around their neighbourhood or travelling to school unaccompanied. The past growth of car ownership made buses less economic to run and so less frequent, making cars yet more necessary.

Feelings about cars are also mixed. For most people, cars are liberating. They allow easy journeys in privacy and are safe, secure, flexible, load-carrying vehicles chosen carefully to fit the lifestyle. Some people are particularly proud to own prestigious marques because of what it says about them. But even for people with low incomes, the car can be a central part of their lives for gaining access to employment and maintaining contact with family and friends, with priority given to car costs in the household budget. For a significant minority—the so-called 'petrol heads'—cars are objects of enthusiasm, the BBC's 'Top Gear' a favourite TV show and its presenter, Jeremy Clarkson, a hero. But for others of a greener disposition, cars are a mixed blessing or even best avoided altogether. Not that the greens are immobile. Rather, growing numbers of people travel with a sense of virtue by bicycle and on increasingly crowded trains.

I explained in Chapter 1 how personal travel has ceased to grow in Britain since the mid-1990s. Journeys by car account for almost 80 per cent of total distance travelled, so it is no surprise that car use per person has also stopped growing. This is not true only for the UK. In the USA vehicle-miles travelled per person ceased to grow after 2000 and have recently been falling significantly. More generally, there is growing evidence that car use per person in a number of developed countries has stagnated recently (discussed in Chapter 1). Given that both travel generally and car use per person are no longer increasing, what now drives the growth of total travel are demographic factors—population growth, urbanisation and increasing longevity.

Planning policy

There has been much debate amongst planners and policy makers about the merits of city versus suburban living. In Britain, a general concern to protect the countryside has led to the adoption of 'green belts' around many cities—areas of countryside where urban sprawl will be resisted. One result has been the movement of people, housing and employment into towns and villages beyond the green belts. This in turn has prompted calls for an urban renaissance, aimed at both protecting the countryside from house building on greenfield sites and preserving the vitality of the central core of cities. In the US, anxieties about inner city dereliction have led to calls for policies to encourage growth in metropolitan areas in the form of more compact communities less dependent on the automobile.

Britain's Labour Government of 1997-2010 was persuaded of the case for inner city revival and encouraged new housing construction on 'brownfield' sites within cities—sites previously used for industrial or commercial use that businesses had abandoned. At the outset, the balance for new housing between greenfield and brownfield was 50:50, so the Government set a modest target of 60 per cent brownfield. In fact, the outcome was nearer 80 per cent, aided by resistance from local inhabitants to greenfield housing developments in their pleasant rural neighbourhoods. But the house-builders were unhappy since greenfield housing was less risky to construct and more profitable to sell. They encouraged the Coalition Government elected in 2010 to review the planning regime. The draft National Planning Policy Framework, issued for consultation, elicited a strong reaction from those concerned with the environment, who thought the floodgates to greenfield housing were to be opened. The Government toned down its proposals in the final version, retaining an apparent preference for brownfield development while dropping the previous specific target.

The question of brownfield versus greenfield is critical for future travel demand and how it is to be met, given expected population growth. The official statisticians project that the population of the UK will increase by an additional five million over the next ten years from the present 63 million, and by ten million by 2035. About half this increase would be the consequence of expected inward migration and about half due to the excess of births over deaths.

Where will these additional citizens live and work? If the necessary housing were constructed on greenfield sites on the edges of existing towns and villages, then it would be inevitable that those who live there will use cars and that the volume of traffic will increase. More traffic would require constructing more road capacity. More cars would mean more impact on the environment from vehicle emissions, in particular the carbon dioxide that contributes to global warming and the fine particulate matter from diesel engines that damages health.

New housing on brownfield sites within existing urban areas, where the scope for extra road space for cars is usually very limited, is best served by public transport. The growth of London's population over the past twenty years was outlined in the previous chapter. There are almost no greenfield sites within the metropolitan area, so population growth has been accommodated by new houses and apartments on previously used sites and through more intensive use of existing properties—subdivision of larger houses into flats, fitting in extra rooms in lofts and rear extensions. The result has been a plateau in the level of car use, and consequently a declining share for the car in the total number of journeys, even as the population has grown.

The relationship between housing and transport can be seen clearly in East London, which is undergoing regeneration as the result of public investment in rail-based travel. The new and revived rail lines through the old Docklands and beyond have prompted extensive private sector investment in new apartment blocks all along these routes. People are willing to live in locations once considered rather remote because these have been made accessible by speedy and reliable rail travel, particularly for the journey to work. It is not only new housing that is changing what were previously the poorer neighbourhoods of East London. The increased access has encouraged people to buy and renovate existing housing, stimulated by prices lower than in more fashionable parts of the capital. Young professionals have been moving east, reviving neighbourhoods that are becoming more diverse in their social composition.

As well as housing, transport investment has made possible a variety of major commercial and public developments in East London, notably London City Airport (suitable for short take-off aircraft), a large exhibition centre, a major entertainment venue, university campuses, the site for the 2012 London Olympic Games and the adjacent large shopping centre, with more such developments expected. In all this, public investment in new transport facilities makes accessible previously hard-to-reach locations which thus creates opportunities for private investment in commercial and residential property. This is how transport investment leads to economic benefits in the form of new jobs and homes.

In contrast to rail investment, road investment has played a smaller role in the regeneration of East London. But roads are important for vans and lorries that deliver goods to work places, shops and homes. Roads are also essential for buses, which can be given a degree of priority in dedicated bus lanes. So for a densely populated city to function effectively, it is necessary to move a substantial proportion of travellers by rail, sufficient to free road space for buses, taxis, freight and emergency vehicles to carry out their tasks unimpeded.

Carbon emissions

The greenfield-brownfield alternatives to accommodate a growing population are also important for combatting climate change. About a quarter of all manmade carbon emissions in Britain derive from transport. The national target is to reduce greenhouse gas emissions to at least 80 per cent below 1990 levels by 2050, to slow global warning. The transport sector, with its reliance on oil for motive power, has been seen as more problematic than other areas of the economy when it comes to reducing carbon emissions. One response is new technology, which I will discuss in Chapter 5.

The way travel demand will develop in the future will be important for the scale of carbon emissions. The flattening off of growth of daily travel per person in the developed economies that I discussed in Chapter 1 is certainly helpful. No doubt the populations of the low-income countries will seek the kind of mobility, access, opportunities and choice from which those of us in the developed economies benefit, but they may not need to follow the same path, as I shall discuss in Chapter 8.

Population growth means more travel, of course. The global population is expected to increase from the present seven billion to reach between eight and eleven billion by 2050. There is also a strong trend to urban living, with future population growth projected to occur entirely in towns and cities. Half of the world's people currently live in urban areas, expected to grow to two-thirds by 2050. Higher population densities in urban areas means that catchment areas—the area sufficiently large to justify investment in a school or a supermarket, for instance—tend to be smaller, allowing more opportunity to walk, cycle or use public transport, rather than use a car. Better public transport can be provided economically where there are larger numbers of users, and more frequent services attract more customers, in a virtuous circle. And there is more scope for using electric-powered vehicles in urban areas where distances are shorter and opportunities for charging points greater.

The growth of transport carbon emissions would be constrained to the extent that growing populations, whether in Britain or globally, are willing to live in relatively dense cities crammed with facilities, but with limited space per person. However, space is attractive, both personal space within the home and green surroundings without the presence of too many other people. So living in the suburbs and beyond will always have an appeal.

Living longer

Nevertheless, it looks as though we may be inclined to live for rather longer in the exciting cities when we are young, delaying the move to the suburbs until rather later in the life course, perhaps prompted by the arrival of a child, or even the second child. The average age of mothers in Britain has been steadily rising, reaching almost 30 years of age for all births in 2011, and 28 years for first births. Nearly two-thirds of fathers were aged 30 and over. A similar pattern is seen in the other countries of Western Europe. This delay in starting a family fits the idea of a prolonged period of career and personal development before 'settling down'. Because we are living longer—with average life expectancy increasing by two years every decade—people in the earlier part of life are taking their time to decide where best to live. As these and other events in the life course are being postponed (with the exception of leaving home), the transition to adulthood occurs both later and becomes more drawn out. Moreover, the increased popularity of living on one's own, unmarried cohabitation and childbirth outside marriage, makes the transition more complex. Indeed, social scientists Francesco Billari and Aart Liefbroer have suggested that a new European pattern of the transition to adulthood is emerging that can be characterized as 'late, protracted and complex', compared with the recent past.

The choice in Britain between city and suburb, brownfield or greenfield, is for most a matter of timing within the life course, the scheduling of the transition from urban experiment to suburban commitment. For a growing number, however, a commitment to urban living in the style common in Europe may be attractive as an alternative to suburbia. It is too early to judge the scale of the trend. Nevertheless, given the magnitude of the existing housing stock, suburban living will continue to be the dominant mode for most of us. But that does not necessarily mean unchanging travel behaviour. Gordon Stokes has found that the older a person is when they learn to drive, the less the annual distance driven—perhaps reflecting experience of using modes other than the car.

Alternatives to the car

There is a movement, a crusade even, to nudge people out of their cars for shorter journeys—more virtuous exercise to counter incipient obesity, less congestion, lower carbon emissions and noxious pollutants. This is particularly relevant for suburban living, where the facilities we need to reach are not so close that we naturally walk, nor so far that the car, if we have one, need be the inevitable option. A marketing approach, in Britain designated 'smarter choices', involves promoting the attractions of alternatives to the car through a variety of mechanisms. Workplace and school travel plans help people think about the various possible ways of getting to these daily destinations other than by car. Personalised travel planning, together with more general information and awareness campaigns, are used by local government to encourage people to consider alternatives to car travel, with the aim of relieving traffic congestion. Car clubs and other kinds of car sharing schemes allow people use of a local car without the expense of sole ownership of a vehicle that typically spends 95 per cent of the time stationary. Car sharing is particularly attractive in inner suburbs where parking space is limited and expensive. One consequence of car sharing is that sharers make fewer car trips overall.

The viability of the bus as an alternative to the car depends on the service—how far you live from a bus stop and how frequently the bus runs. Some operators have been innovative, opening new routes to meet demand, often with small vehicles. However, a basic issue for bus transport is the population density of the area served. Low density means lower frequency services, since it is not economic to run largely empty buses. But low frequency is unattractive to users who will prefer the car if they have one, which further reduces the viability of the route.

There is, nevertheless, scope to configure bus services to cater for off-peak, cross-city and recreational travel, as well as peak flows. A network of routes, linking with rail and trams, and with easy transfers, can attract passengers—as seen in many European cities as well as London. There is a 'network effect' at work—recognised by economists as a 'positive externality'—in which the more users there are, the greater the value for each user, as first seen in the early days of telephones. For buses what is needed is a single planned network with near effortless transfers between routes, with timetable coordination and through ticketing.

There is a debate about how best to organise a bus network. The approach in Britain outside London is to allow bus companies to run the routes they wish, hoping that competition between them will lead to services that meet people's needs. However, experience has shown that private operators rarely find it profitable to compete to meet demand on the same route, so the benefits of competition are limited. In contrast in London, Transport for London, a public body overseen by the Mayor, plans the network and collects the fares, but operation of individual bus routes is contracted out to private sector companies.

While bus use in London has been buoyant, outside London patronage has generally declined, although there are exceptions such as Oxford, Cambridge, Brighton, Nottingham, York and Edinburgh where high population density (including students) and good local managers are able to buck the general trend. The experience of London suggests that coordination and integration of operations across a whole city, centre and suburbs, results in a better service than on-the-road competition. The other attributes that promote bus use are clean, well-maintained, modern vehicles; stability of service; simple fare structure; low floor buses to reduce boarding time; the requirement to purchase tickets before boarding, to reduce delays and improve reliability; passenger information at stops, real time displays of arrival time and location; bus priority lanes; and comprehensive evening and weekend services.

Coordination of services is also the arrangement found in European cities with high quality public transport systems. Only where population density and demand is exceptionally high, as in Hong Kong, are competing bus services compatible with high levels of service.

Digital substitutes

As well as the replacements to the car for travel, there are alternatives to making a journey in the first place, whether to work, to meetings or to the shops. These involve taking advantage of information and telecommunications technology—digital technologies—particularly teleworking, video-conferencing and online shopping. In general, such technologies could substitute for travel, could facilitate it, or could modify travel behaviour—for instance by freeing up a car that could be used by someone else in the household for some other purpose. All these possibilities can be observed on a modest scale as yet, but with growing impact. The longer-term implications remain unclear.

Teleworking seems to have made a limited impression so far on the number of journeys to work. In Britain, only five per cent of us usually work at home. Video-conferencing has also made only a small impact as yet, although there is substantial potential for growth, taking advantage of the increasing availability of high quality hardware for business meetings and of low cost Internet-based communication such as Skype. The question is whether this is likely to affect the amount of travel. To what extent can remote contact substitute for meeting face-to-face? Or perhaps ease of communication helps people build bigger networks of friends and colleagues with whom they'll want to meet with when they can, not least for informal contact over food and drink to cultivate understanding and trust. There is some suggestion that the availability of electronic communication may be allowing people to travel a bit less, but the effect is not great as yet. When the Internet arrived in the mid-1990s, many predicted the decline of cities—why live in a scruffy city when you could work in the beautiful countryside? The opposite seems to be happening. Cities are becoming more popular, their inhabitants lured by social networks and chance encounters that make life richer. Smartphones are helping make dense cities good places to live and digital technology is changing behaviour, including travel behaviour.

Online shopping is growing rapidly, both through wholly new businesses like Amazon (initially for books but now for a wide range of consumer goods) and delivery-only supermarkets like Ocado in Britain, but also as established stores develop their own websites and delivery arrangements. In the US, some eight per cent of all retail sales were recently estimated to be online, with growth of ten per cent a year expected. Online shopping is advancing in Britain, where population density makes delivery relatively cheap and where broadband Internet access is general. 75 per cent of households now order goods by phone, post or over the Internet, up from 65 per cent ten years ago. The growth of online shopping has been largely at the expense of ordering by phone or post, however. Ten years ago, three-quarters of such orders were by post or phone, with only one quarter via the Internet, but now this ratio is reversed, with 75 per cent placed online. The consequences of the impact of the growth of online shopping on travel have been small so far. However, the potential for further online growth is substantial and relevant for travel demand since one delivery van might substitute for 30 or more individual shopping trips a day. On the other hand, the practice of collecting goods ordered online from a store—'click and collect'— is also growing, which does not reduce shopping trips. There has been a long-term decline in the frequency of shopping in Britain, largely due to longer trips by car substituting for more frequent trips on foot. Online shopping may prolong this trend.

Smarter choices

Digital alternatives to car travel complement efforts to change behaviour by means of the 'smarter choices' approach, proponents of which claim that traffic reduction of some ten per cent is possible. What limits this is that the alternatives to the car tend to be slower, so that access and choice are reduced. You may be willing to give up the car if your journey to work could be readily managed by public transport or bike. But if you are thinking of changing jobs, you might not want your choice to be limited by a prior decision to avoid car travel, and if the best new job on offer requires car to get there, then that's probably what you'll do. On the other hand, for someone else a change of employment might bring them nearer home, making alternatives to the car more feasible. Cars and vans are responsible for nearly 60 per cent of all journeys to work in Britain because their use allows much more choice of jobs accessible within reasonable time from where people live. So the scope for reducing car trips to work is inevitably limited.

Another limitation on the smarter choices approach is that the road space freed up by encouraging some people to give up the car is likely to be taken advantage of by others not so persuaded. Reducing car use at time of peak travel would reduce congestion and speed up the traffic. Faster travel tends to encourage longer trips, as people take advantage of higher speed to extend access and choice, as described in Chapter 1. Accordingly, it is generally accepted that to 'lock in' the traffic reduction arising from smarter choices initiatives, it is necessary to put in place some 'hard' measures, the effect of which cannot be avoided, such as reduction in road space for cars through more pavement for pedestrians or more lanes for buses and bicycles. Other possibilities are adjusting traffic signals to constrain traffic, and congestion charging, as in central London. Of course, if you reduce road space for cars you don't get the benefit of congestion reduction, although you do achieve reduced carbon emissions.

Whatever measures adopted to lock in the traffic reduction, the question that remains is why bother with the 'soft' smarter choice measures, given it is the 'hard' constraints that do the job? In London, where the share of journeys by car is on a long-run downward trend, as explained in Chapter 2, it has been the 'hard' impact of limited road space that has been responsible, with more pedestrian space particularly popular. Smarter choice measures aimed at changing behaviour have not been important in London. Generally, measures aimed at changing behaviour are best seen as a way of marketing alternatives to the car to people who may not be aware of these, particularly in circumstances where they are conscious of limitations on car use, such as regular traffic congestion or parking restrictions.

Regardless of the merits of attempting to nudge people out of their cars in the higher density suburbs, the possibilities of doing this are minimal in the lower density 'exurbs' that surround many US cities and in rural areas generally. Distances increase, traffic speeds rise (bad for cyclists), and public transport is less frequent or absent altogether. The car becomes essential for rural living if opportunities are not to be sacrificed.

Ageing populations

Rural life appeals to many, particularly to those active after retirement. Car-based mobility works well for them, at least until the minor disabilities of later life build up. Small losses of sight, hearing, dexterity and reaction time cumulatively induce people to restrict and eventually abandon driving, which can leave them feeling stranded. With an ageing population, we need to plan to maintain mobility after the car.

The ageing of the population arises from two main developments: longevity is increasing, and the baby boom generation is approaching later life. Greater longevity allows the young to take their time before settling down, as discussed earlier. The implications of a larger cohort of older people, the baby boomers, might be forecast on the assumption that their travel behaviour would be similar to earlier cohorts, allowing for trends such as the increase in the proportion of older women holding a driving licence. However, life expectancy has been growing rapidly—in Britain increasing by more than two years per decade recently—and is projected to continue to increase in the coming years. The question that arises concerns the propensity to travel in these extra years of later life. And this depends importantly on health status.

Debate continues about whether late life disability is increasing or decreasing. The balance of evidence suggests that deterioration is being postponed, so that levels of health that used to be prevalent at age 70 now are found at age 80. One implication is that people will continue to drive until more advanced ages, given the attractions of the car for gaining easy access to desired destinations. However, the larger baby boom cohort will mean greater numbers reaching the point when people give up driving on account of the cumulative impact of minor disabilities. Mobility is important for quality of life. Loss of mobility in later life is detrimental not just in respect of access to destinations, but also loss of the incidental benefits—getting out and about, exercise and social engagement. Moreover, loss of outdoors mobility tends to trigger general functional decline. Population ageing therefore has implications for travel demand and for transport provision. The growing proportion of older women able to drive allows the convenience of car-based mobility for more people in later life, which increases the impact of a key decision—the timing of giving up driving. Alternative means of mobility and access are then needed, the demand for which will increase as the population ages.

In Britain, one response has been the provision of free off-peak travel on buses for older people (on all public transport in London). The historic trend to increasing car ownership and licence holding by the over 60s contributed importantly to the decline in bus use outside London, but free bus use is now helping to reverse this trend by encouraging people to try out public transport in place of the car to which they have become accustomed. It also has wider social benefits, including encouraging minding of grandchildren and volunteering. But recourse to the bus in place of the car only works where there are reasonably frequent buses services, which is not the case in rural areas. An alternative approach that is growing in the US, where bus services are generally limited, takes the form of a taxi service employing volunteer drivers, with bookings made on a custom software system that is franchised to individual communities.

Another response to an ageing population no longer able to drive cars is the growing use of pavement-running mobility scooters, well suited to preserving personal mobility in urban areas for those who find walking difficult. The trend to create more space for pedestrians in urban areas is helpful for those using scooters as well as for the general population on foot. These electric-powered vehicles, operating at up to eight miles per hour, are supplied by a large number of manufacturers. Unlike other kinds of powered transport, there has not so far been consolidation of the sector into a limited number of well-known manufacturers whose reputation attests to the quality of the product. Nor have we seen the implementation of regulations governing safety and performance. Given the potential growth in demand as the population ages, there is a market opportunity for some of the existing car and motorbike manufactures to develop a range of high quality, price-competitive scooters.

So rather than retire to a rural village, a better choice is a prosperous market town, seaside resort or mature suburb with good public transport and with facilities close enough for walking, or, if our legs fail us, to reach on our scooter.

The aim of this chapter has been to argue that what will determine the demand for travel in future in a developed economy is increasingly demographic and geographic factors—a growing and ageing population, and where we choose to live over the course of our longer lives. On the whole, a shift towards quality urban environments of sufficient density that the car is not essential seems good for younger people who enjoy active work and social lives, as well as for older people no longer able to drive. It is also good for the environment.

Chapter Four

Going Global

Travelling faster over long distances has transformed our perception of the planet. Columbus took five weeks to sail across the Atlantic Ocean. The opening of the transcontinental railway across the US, the linking of Indian railways across the subcontinent, and the opening of the Suez Canal, all in 1869-70, inspired Jules Verne to write *Around-the-World in Eighty Days*. Thomas Cook arranged his first roundtheworld trip in 1872, the beginning of organised tourism. Nowadays trans-Atlantic flight takes eight hours, and we can fly from the UK to Australia in less than a day.

Unlike daily travel, long distance trips are mostly irregular, take significant chunks of time and are the result of particular decisions. Most air travel is for leisure purposes—tourism, visiting family and friends. Business travel is economically important but a minority of trips. Affordable air travel, together with inexpensive telecommunications, has made possible not just tourism but also migration while retaining family ties (trans-national families) and community links (diasporas). Cities like London become 'world cities' by virtue of the global connections of both businesses and the population of residents, whether settled or temporary.

As trade barriers diminish and financial capital flows to take advantage of investment opportunities, so we get globalisation in the form of increased volumes of trade and cross-border investment. In contrast, labour flows are generally very restricted, with the exception of the European Union where borders are open to those who wish to work in another member state.

Migration

Migrants are varied. There are temporary workers, for instance those in seasonal employment in agriculture, and professionals who migrate, both for training and to work for limited periods in branches of trans-national companies. Other workers are unauthorised—those working illegally, which in Europe may amount to as much as one per cent of the national population. There are refugees and asylum seekers escaping natural catastrophes or persecution. Most countries welcome, to varying degrees, permanent settlers with useful skills; such settlers typically bring family members, which for the UK comprise a third of all immigrants and as much as 70 per cent in the US.

There are economic motives driving migration. Individuals aim to better themselves. Families seek insurance and remittances by sending a member to work abroad. Land shortage, environmental damage and other pressures from growing populations in originating countries induce migration. These pressures also result in internal movement from rural areas to cities, where urbanisation facilitates subsequent migration overseas. The willingness of migrants to do jobs in receiving countries that the locals are reluctant to undertake—those that are dirty, dangerous, difficult and poorly paid—ensures a welcome from employers of this kind of labour. Migrants tend to be healthier, more capable and enterprising, the people their countries can least afford to lose. But they may be seen as heroes on account of the remittances they send home, as well as the skills and capital they bring if they return. Immigrants do not necessarily start work at the bottom of the heap. Well-educated Chinese migrate across the Pacific to seek economic security while maintaining businesses in China and elsewhere in Asia, and migrants to Silicon Valley from a number of countries return home with expertise to start new enterprises.

Constraints on migration take the form of visa requirements, although when these are abandoned, as within the European Union, flows of people to take advantage of employment opportunities can be substantial. The Poles who migrated to the UK after Poland's accession to the EU now number half million, making Polish the second main language in Britain after English.

The scale of international migration is likely to grow in the future. The global population is growing, increasing pressures to emigrate from poorer countries. Environmental degradation, arising from both population growth and climate change, adds to this pressure. The ageing of the population in developed countries opens possibilities for inward migration, both of those skilled in care provision, and more generally of younger workers. Ease of travel and communication makes migration more attractive for migrants and harder to resist by recipient populations.

Migrants tend to congregate and establish networks. A pioneer settles perhaps arbitrarily in a particular place and sends word back if there are employment possibilities, which triggers a chain of migration. Communities and networks form with roots in both the home country and the new country, where the first generation children are born. They make good use of cheap flights to regional airports to keep in touch with families at home.

Travel arising from migration is much more important than travel by migrants initially migrating. Of the 31 million visitors to Britain in 2011, almost nine million were visiting family and friends. There has been a five-fold increase in the number of seats on aircraft between Poland and Britain since Poland entered the EU. And of the 57 million trips by UK residents who travelled abroad, over eleven million were to visit friends and relatives. As the world globalises, as families proliferate across national borders, so international travel seems set to grow inexorably.

Figure 2. Passengers through UK airport terminals

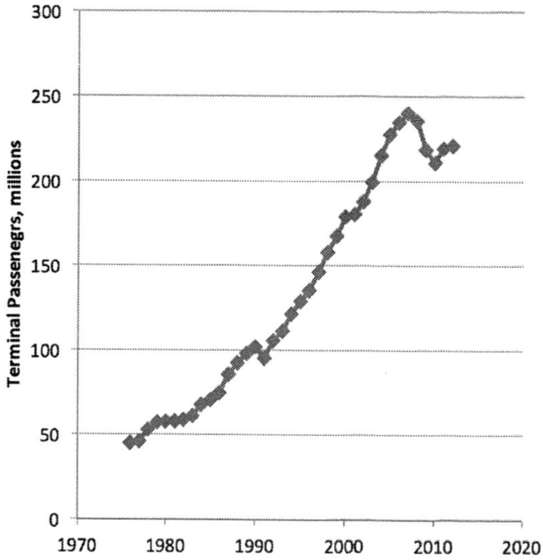

Demand for air travel

But is air travel certain to grow in the future? Three-quarters of all passenger travel to and from Britain is by air. Air travel has grown hugely since the 1970s. Passengers using UK airports increased from 45 million in 1976 to reach a peak of 240 million in 2007, since when numbers have fallen back, to 220 million in 2012 (see Figure 2). The question is to what extent this break in the long-term growth trend is a temporary consequence of the economic recession, and to what extent it may reflect a saturation of demand for air travel. Recall that I proposed saturation of demand for daily travel in Chapter 1. Is something similar emerging for air travel?

UK residents on average make rather less than one return journey by air a year. However, surveys show that just over half the population do not fly in any one year—call these the 'infrequent flyers'. Frequency of air travel increases from lower to higher socio-economic status, is higher for younger people, lower for older people, and rises with income. Even so, around a quarter those in the top social group or in the highest fifth of incomes took no flights in the previous year. The prospects for the growth of demand for air travel depend importantly on whether these infrequent flyers are likely to change their habits in the future.

The group of infrequent flyers is pretty mixed. Some people have never flown. Some fly rarely or only occasionally. Others regularly take annual holidays abroad but may have missed a year for a particular reason such as illness. Some current infrequent flyers may have flown frequently in an earlier phase of life. Surveys of passengers using UK airports show that over the past ten years, less than one per cent are flying for the first time. This indicates that much of the growth in passenger traffic in recent years has come from existing passengers travelling more often. The implication is that those of the infrequent flyers who have never flown may be unlikely to change their habits.

The future behaviour of the infrequent flyers is one source of uncertainty for future demand for air travel. A further uncertainty is how many more trips those who regularly fly might make. Time invariably limits travel, whether daily travel constrained by the tasks to be done within the 24hour day, or, for flying, time away from home or office, or time available for vacations. It is very possible that the time most of us have for longer trips abroad by air is approaching its limit. Short trips on weekend breaks can more readily be fitted in. Much of the recent growth of air travel has been due to the availability of low cost flights that make such trips affordable, albeit involving disproportionate amounts of time spent tediously at airports. One group that is not time-limited is older people who can take advantage of retirement to spend periods in holiday homes abroad. An increasingly ageing population may mean more older flyers. On the other hand, prospects for pensions are worsening, which would constrain both owning overseas properties and taking trips abroad.

Altogether, there is a lot of uncertainty about the future demand for air travel by UK residents. The likely future behaviour of both the infrequent and regular flyers needs to be investigated because it is important for understanding future demand for air travel, a central consideration in planning additional airport capacity. Changes in attitudes to flying and the effect of time constraints are disregarded in conventional econometric analysis used to inform demand forecasts, where it is assumed that behaviour does not change except where driven by parameters that are explicitly modelled such as income or fares.

Airport development

Assumptions implicit in demand forecasts are particularly relevant to the continuing debate about airport development in southeast England. The main London airport at Heathrow has only two runways and is operating to capacity at times of peak demand. While the airlines and business travellers press for a further runway, those who live nearby strongly resist on account of noise and pollution. Some argue for a wholly new airport on the Thames Estuary to replace Heathrow. The political parties vacillate and the government procrastinates because the decision is particularly difficult. An independent commission has been set up to consider the issues. My concern is that what is common to most those involved in this debate is the supposition that the demand for air travel to and from Britain is set to grow substantially—but, as I have explained, this is far from certain.

The usual approach to decisions about new airport capacity may be termed 'predict and provide'. Predict the demand—in this case, growth in passenger numbers—and then provide the capacity. This is a sensible way of thinking about infrastructure investment for the utilities such as electricity, gas, water and telecommunications. It used to be the philosophy underpinning plans for new road construction in Britain, at least until the announcement of a major programme of road building in 1989 triggered a strong public backlash from those not wanting to see more countryside concreted over. The Newbury Bypass, built in 1995-98 after vigorous resistance by protestors, was probably the last new major road to be constructed across greenfield land. So the philosophy then changed to 'demand management'. We could not build our way out of congestion, it was generally agreed, so we would need to manage demand for road travel (more on this in Chapter 6). The main idea for achieving this is 'road pricing', also known as 'congestion charging' and implemented in central London. By charging for use of road space, particularly when congested with traffic, some people decide not to travel, or to travel at others times, leaving more room for those who travel needs are more pressing.

Air travel already uses something like demand management to set fares—known as 'yield management', the now familiar flexible pricing introduced by the budget airlines and adopted generally for shorthaul flights. This allows the airlines to offer bargain prices on less popular flights and to those who can book early, and to make an acceptable overall return by charging more for popular routes, busy times and late bookers.

Demand management through flexible fares would allow the sensible development of air travel in the face of constrained capacity at Heathrow. A key argument for expansion of Heathrow is the increasing demand for business travel, which is generally supposed to be important for economic growth. However, passengers on business trips are a minority at UK airports, less than a quarter of the total—half of these are British residents flying out, half foreign residents flying in. Three-quarters of airport users are travelling for leisure. Even at Heathrow, 70 per cent of passengers are travelling for leisure rather than business.

There is therefore ample airport capacity for increased business travel by air, including at Heathrow, by displacing leisure travellers. Business travellers would generally be prepared to pay a price premium for a convenient airport or one that acts as a hub for picking up long-haul flights. A market in landing and take-off opportunities ('slots', as they are known) is developing which would facilitate preferential allocation to flights catering substantially for business travellers. An increase in airport charges, which are set by the Civil Aviation Authority (the industry regulator) could encourage point-to-point leisure travellers, who do not need to change aircraft at a hub, to switch to other airports with spare capacity—including regional airports beyond south-east England.

To illustrate the implications, consider flights between UK airports and Nice airport in the South of France, a popular destination for both leisure and business travellers. The 1.5 million travellers in 2011 used sixteen UK airports, including all the airports in the London area. 35 per cent flew via Heathrow, but it is likely that a large proportion of these were UK residents travelling point-to-point and who could therefore have used an alternative airport, and indeed would have done so had a significant price differential existed.

From the UK passenger's point of view, there are generally acceptable alternatives to Heathrow for short-haul leisure flights, and also alternative hubs with plenty of capacity for transfer to long-haul flights—such as at Amsterdam, Paris, Frankfurt and Madrid, which are indeed increasingly used by

UK residents in the north of England and Scotland. Moreover, it is often substantially cheaper to fly to a long-haul destination from the UK via a European, Middle Eastern or US hub than to fly direct from Heathrow. So the business travellers whose time is scarce fly direct, while leisure travellers, paying for themselves for longer vacations, are willing to incur the additional time changing planes—all of which makes good economic sense.

The increased utilisation of airport capacity at the Heathrow hub for business travellers, by displacing some leisure travellers, would allow increased connectivity to new destinations in developing economies. This would be helped by the use of larger aircraft such as the Airbus 380 on busy routes, terminal capacity being easier to increase than runway capacity.

It is not only UK residents that use UK airports. There are inward travellers as well, including growing numbers of the middle classes of developing economies who are travelling abroad. On the other hand, travel to the UK by US residents has not increased over the past twenty years, while travel from Japan has fallen substantially over this period, evidence for market maturity that likely reflects economic and demographic trends—including the ageing of the Japanese population

Generally, first time visitors to Britain will want to visit the main historic sites of London, the capacity of which may be approaching their practical limit. London is already the most visited city in the world, with 20 million visitors a year. The free-to-enter British Museum is the most visited attraction in Britain, on the itinerary of one in four overseas visitors to London, and uncomfortably crowded for most of the year. London coped with the visitors to the 2012 Olympic Games only by discouraging normal tourists in that year and by encouraging Londoners to adjust their travel patterns. To build Britain's tourism business, it could be more attractive to market to European repeat visitors who could use regional airports to travel beyond London.

It would be sensible to explore the implications of low demand growth for air travel when considering the rather difficult decisions about additional airport capacity in south-east England. There are serious environmental impediments to enlarging the existing airports in a densely populated region, and likewise to building a new airport within easy reach of the capital. It is possible that we could manage with the capacity we have. London is thriving with a major transport capacity constraint—a fixed amount of road capacity that has led to a declining share of journeys by car as the population has grown. But this has not proved to be a problem. The work-around has been to invest in public transport. For air travel, the work-around is to prioritise business travel at Heathrow—which would happen naturally if the market were allowed to operate—displacing short-haul leisure travellers to smaller airports, and perhaps displacing some altogether. For instance, the hen and stag parties who fly abroad for weekends at low cost destinations would be unlikely to enjoy themselves much less at British resorts.

Freight

Cheap fast personal air travel plays a big part in globalisation, for business travellers, migrants and their families and friends. Speeding up of freight transport, both faster ships and airfreight, has also been central to the globalisation process—space only for brief mention in a book concerned about personal travel.

Two hundred years ago, goods moved slowly, horse-drawn on poor roads and canals, or in slow sailing ships. The advent of steam power transformed world trade, starting early in the nineteenth century. The invention of telecommunications early in the twentieth century contributed further impetus. The recent move of much manufacturing to the Far East has meant a big shift to service sector businesses for the UK economy, for which travel, transport and telecoms are crucial.

The last leg of global freight movement is always by road to your home or a nearby shop. Road freight movements by heavy goods vehicles have not grown in Britain since the mid-1990s, suggesting the end of an era in which rising prosperity depended on moving ever-larger amounts of weighty stuff. With digitisation and miniaturisation of consumer goods, increasingly delivered to your front door, now is the era of the Light Goods Vehicle or 'white van'. While car use per capita has ceased to grow, LGV use continues to increase, in part as consequence of home deliveries from online shopping, with a net transport saving when individual car trips to the supermarket are replaced by a delivery van serving many households. More generally, while people can switch from car to public transport or bikes, this is not possible for freight, so it is to be expected that LGV use will grow at least in line with population increase, even in London.

Freight transport is a complicated topic where data is limited and generalisations not easy. Nevertheless, we need not assume that demand for freight transport in the developed economies is set to grow faster than the population grows. As with air travel, the market may be more mature than is generally supposed, and, as with personal daily travel, we may have reached the end of the era of per capita growth for goods—the end of the third era of travel.

Chapter Five:

Speed Limits

Two hundred years ago we moved at walking pace or not much faster, on foot, in carts and carriages on poor roads, and on water—canal, river and sea. Horizons were limited. Then began two centuries of innovation in transport technologies, a crucial contribution to the economic and social developments that characterise our modern world. The key breakthrough was harnessing the energy-dense fossil fuels, initially coal and subsequently oil, to increase the power available for movement beyond that of a team of horses.

First came the steam engine, generating power by burning coal to boil water into steam, which took over from water-power to turn the wheels of the early factories and made the Industrial Revolution possible. Then the steam engine was put to work to propel trains with steel wheels on smooth, even steel rails—much more efficient than cart wheels on rough roads—and the nineteenth century railway boom began.

Over the course of that century road construction techniques were improved to allow horse-drawn vehicles to travel faster, and later bicycles and motor vehicles. The modern, mass-produced motorcar first hit the road just a century ago in the form of the Model T Ford. Since then, a succession of incremental refinements from intensely competitive manufacturers has brought the car to its present high level of performance, comfort and reliability. Manufacturing costs have been reducing in real terms so that a large proportion of households in developed economies own a car, with those in developing countries having similar aspirations.

Car technology

For the future, the main challenge for the car manufacturers is to reduce emissions of carbon dioxide and noxious pollutants by improving the efficiency of conventional technologies and developing new forms of propulsion, principally using electricity derived from low-carbon sources. The leading manufacturers are putting a lot of effort into improving electric and hybrid cars to meet the needs of drivers at acceptable cost, although there is some way to go before the price of such vehicles becomes appealing to most motorists. Electric-only cars have attractions, in particular simplicity and efficiency. However, the weight of the batteries to store a given amount of energy is some 25 times that of petrol, which limits vehicle performance. While the range of electric cars is generally sufficient for most daily driving, these vehicles at present seem unattractive for longer trips, given the uncertainty of available recharging locations and the time taken to recharge. But much research is aimed at improving battery technology, which may in time enhance vehicle performance, driver perceptions and market potential. Current batteries deliver only about a quarter of the energy storage potential of their active ingredients, so there is room for substantial improvement.

Hybrid vehicles have both an electric motor and an internal combustion engine. The former, when run in reverse, allows regenerative braking—capturing energy otherwise wasted when the vehicle slows down to charge the batteries. Plug-in hybrids have the advantage that they can be charged overnight from cheap mains electricity. While the range using the battery is limited, the internal combustion engine ensures that travel is not constrained by recharging opportunities, thus avoiding the 'range anxiety' associated with electric-only cars.

There is also some effort to develop hydrogen-powered fuel cells as an onboard source of electric power instead of a battery. Some buses in a number of cities use this technology, which generates zero carbon and pollutant emissions from the vehicle. For wide application, however, it would be necessary to invest in a system for the storage and distribution of hydrogen gas, technically and economically a major undertaking, so the prospects seem limited.

In a standard oil-fuelled car only 25 per cent of the energy is used for movement, while some 75 per cent is lost in heating the engine and radiator. So one strategy for consuming less energy and emitting less carbon is to make the energy-conversion chain more efficient. Smaller, lighter vehicles help, as does streamlining to reduce air resistance, engine stop-start for urban crawling, low rolling resistance tyres, turbochargers and downsized engines. Development of conventional technologies often proves to be a cheaper means to improvement than new technology, and responses to environmental regulation through technological ingenuity are frequently less costly than anticipated, as is proving to be the case for carbon reduction from vehicles.

While there is a lot of effort devoted to improving vehicle performance and reducing carbon and other emissions, what is *not* happening is effort to devise road vehicles that would go significantly faster. The energy needed to propel a vehicle rises rapidly as the speed increases, roughly with the cube of the velocity. Energy is needed to overcome both the resistance of the air through which it moves and internal friction within the engine. So if speed is doubled, energy use increases eightfold. Carbon, other noxious emissions and noise increase with energy use. And safety concerns grow with speed. So, if anything, lower speeds for vehicles on urban roads seem more likely than higher speeds. Moreover, oil as a fuel is non-renewable, and while there is no shortage of reserves, there are limited amounts of cheap oil available, so its price is on an upward trend long-term. Vehicle carbon emissions are subject to increasingly stringent regulatory limits, driven by concerns about climate change. For all these reasons there is unlikely to be any significant increase of vehicle speeds on uncongested roads.

Rail technology

The prospects for higher speeds look poor generally in the transport sector, with the possible exception of high-speed rail, with trains capable of speeds over 200 mph on dedicated track, as are now common in Europe. This technology was pioneered in Japan with the Shinkansen train between Tokyo and Osaka, which started operations in the 1960s. France came next with the TGV, now an extensive network, and the other major western European countries followed. There has been debate in the US about the possible role for high-speed rail but no decisions to build as yet.

There is certainly a case for constructing more rail capacity in Britain, given growing passenger demand that has doubled since the low point in the early 1900s, as well as projected population growth. There is an argument that if you are going to construct additional inter-urban rail routes, it would be sensible to adopt the highest speed technology currently available, even though this technology looks expensive in relation to the benefits (as I shall discuss in Chapter 6). But to attain usefully reduced journey times, the number of stations on a route must be limited. This tends to result in discontent on the part of inhabitants of areas that suffer from the deleterious impact of a new route without having a nearby station to compensate—although the extra capacity can reduce crowding on existing commuting routes. In any event, rail represents a minority of all trips in Britain, and high-speed rail a minority of a minority, so the impact on the overall average speed of travel will be quite limited.

Magnetic levitation—trains without wheels floating over the track by magnetic repulsion—allows speeds of over 300 mph, but the technology is demanding and costly, with only a few small systems in operation worldwide. The Maglev that connects Shanghai airport to the edge of the city centre takes only eight minutes, but is much more expensive than the slower metro which serves the whole city. These trains use special tracks, which makes the technology inflexible, unlike high-speed rail where trains can use standard tracks for parts of journeys.

While new generations of aircraft are expected to be more economical in fuel use, they are not expected to travel faster. The supersonic Concorde proved to be a technological dead end, burning too much fuel, too noisy and too costly to build and operate, for the benefit of too few flyers willing to pay premium fares. Generally, there has been no increase in aircraft speed since the introduction of the Boeing 707 in 1958. But better fuel economy has allowed increases in range, lessening the need for refuelling stops on long-haul flights and so reducing travel time.

So we have come to the end of an era of growth in travel, not just because we now have high levels of access, opportunities and choice as I argued earlier, but also because we have largely run out of possibilities for travelling faster by means of new technologies. Transport technologies, both vehicles, infrastructure and the associated fuel supply technologies, are mutually locked in, one with another, and are therefore slow to evolve, unlike innovations based on electronics. Transport technologies are inherently very substantial, so it takes huge investments to make changes, unlike weightless software operating on ever miniaturising digital devices.

Traffic congestion

There remains the possibility of travelling faster on the roads if we could effectively tackle traffic congestion. The obvious answer seems to build more road capacity, at least where there is land available that is not already built upon. This means widening busy motorways on the periphery of conurbations, where there is both a lot of traffic and land for extra lanes. But we find in practice that such new road capacity fills up pretty quickly with extra traffic—and congestion is restored to what it was. Consider the M25 orbital motorway around the edge of London. About half of the traffic is long distance, for instance from south coast ports to the Midlands avoiding central London. The other half is local traffic, people travelling to work and making other trips, taking advantage of a segment of the motorway to speed their journeys. Road widening at first allows higher speeds at peak hours and so permits people to travel a bit further for more choice of jobs and homes, as I explained in Chapter 1. As a result, pressures arise to develop land in or near the Green Belt around London for housing or commercial use, which may or may not be a good thing depending on your point of view.

The extra distances travelled by car to and from both existing and new developments result additional traffic—known as 'induced traffic', the consequence of the extra capacity. There was once debate about whether road construction created more traffic. Those keen on road building were in denial since the extra traffic would reduce the time saving that was supposed to be the main benefit of new construction. But it is now clear that the benefit is taken as longer distances travelled, which results in additional carbon and other emissions, noise and accidents, with no congestion reduction in the long run on account of the extra traffic.

So widening the M25 and similar sections of busy motorway in effect amounts to enlarging the capacity of a local distributor road in the neighbourhood of a conurbation. This permits local property development at the cost of greater traffic volumes, while offering little benefit for the performance of long distance traffic. In contrast, when the motorway system was originally constructed, the impact nationally was very substantial. For instance, higher speeds of travel allowed the supply chains for retail branches of national firms to be rationalised. Regional warehouses were closed and stocks consolidated into huge distribution depots located in the centre of the country, from which three-quarters of retail stores could be supplied in a round trip within the day. This saved both inventory and warehouse space, reduced costs, and improved the reliability of supply. However, these benefits can only be taken once, and so this phase of logistics rationalisation has largely concluded. We now have a mature road network, with few plans for any wholly new roads. Adding an additional lane at very considerable expense, as with the M25 widening, is poor value, as are the schemes for 'managed motorways' that involve use of the hard shoulders as an additional traffic lane under congested condition, subject to reduced speed limits. The benefits of road improvements are now very modest. For instance, an evaluation of 58 major schemes recently implemented by the Highways Agency (responsible for England's motorways and trunk roads) found time savings to road users at peak usage of only three minutes on average.

Another approach to tackling traffic congestion is by charging for using the road, which deters some drivers who either don't make the trip or are deflected to an alternative route. Tolled motorways are familiar in parts of Europe and the US, where the revenues are used to finance construction, maintenance and operation of the road. In Britain, tolled roads are limited to some river crossings and the short M6 Toll near Birmingham, which allows long-distance traffic a congestion-free route since the charge of around £5 deters local traffic. Tolled roads can be acceptable when they are new constructions and the old roads remain available for those who do not wish to pay. There is usually considerable public resistance to introducing charges for existing roads, however.

One place where such charges have been introduced successfully for existing roads is the congestion charging zone in Central London, which drivers pay £10 a day to enter. There was initially a noticeable effect on congestion, although this has tended to decline over time. Other cities that have adopted road pricing include Stockholm, Milan and Singapore. There are also toll roads in the US that are free to high-occupancy vehicles and can be used by unaccompanied drivers for a charge that varies according to the volume of traffic.

Economists are generally keen on road charging as a logical means for rationing a scarce resource—road capacity at times of peak demand. However, the point of charging for road use is to deter those for whom the benefit of the journey no longer outweighs the cost, which means that low-income motorists tend to be most affected. This makes road pricing unpopular with the voters, so the prospects for general adoption look unpromising.

I conclude that the case for widening motorways to speed long distance traffic is unpersuasive; and the case for introducing road pricing generally is politically difficult. In any event, growth of motorway traffic generally is now quite modest in Britain, indeed has been flat in recent years on account of the recession. As I explained in previous chapters, car use per capita on all roads has ceased to grow and the trend of heavy goods vehicle use is no longer rising, indeed has declined in the last few years. Large numbers for the cost of congestion in Britain—from £7 billion to £30 billion—are bandied about, but they lack a reliable basis. Such costs are typically voiced by bodies like industry trade associations seeking an issue that is uncontentious amongst their diverse membership. There are, in fact, reasons to suppose that the cost of unanticipated congestion is quite small for operators who understand the road network. This points to a better way of managing demand for road travel.

Efficient road freight operators under contract with the supermarket chains for long distance transport between central depots and stores typically have to deliver within 30-minute time slots or face a penalty—an example of what is known as 'just in time delivery'. This they can achieve because they know the location and control the progress of each vehicle and understand where traffic congestion arises. I had the opportunity to ask a senior executive of a well-known freight haulier to what extent unanticipated congestion affected performance. His memorable response was that it had less impact than unanticipated delays at customers' premises. More generally, congestion in Britain is responsible for only about a quarter of delays in road freight transport, and the logistics operators are acquiring the skills to manage this better using advances in digital technologies.

When you ask road users generally why congestion is a problem, the main concern is not that travel is slower than it might be. What is more bothering is the uncertainty of arrival time. One approach to dealing with this primary consequence of congestion is to tackle it directly by providing drivers with good predictions of journey times before they set out, so that they can plan to arrive on time. Those who are flexible can delay their start until peak congestion has abated, so reducing congestion for those who can't delay—a 'win-win' situation and a very acceptable form of demand management. A nice example is the website of the Department of Transportation of Washington State in the USA which shows real time traffic conditions on the main routes in the Seattle region. For the regular user, a glance indicates the degree of congestion. This website also allows commuters to determine their time to leave home to arrive at work on time for nineteen out of twenty journeys. Another website goes further in that it predicts traffic conditions an hour ahead on the current day and also for future days on the Autobahns of North-Rhine Westphalia, Germany.

Suppliers of in-car satellite navigation route guidance now provide real time traffic information about delays, optimal routes and estimated time of arrival, derived from roadside monitors, in-vehicle devices and drivers' mobile phones, and may propose alternative routes. Apps for mobile phones provide similar information. A further service that should be feasible is information about parking availability in urban areas. For the future, advances in traffic sensing, modelling and prediction mean that 'predictive navigation' will supersede the existing Satnav devices that have become so popular.

Providing drivers with information about predicted journey times, to allow them to cope with congestion, is better than resorting to road pricing to speed traffic flows. In general, road pricing reduces congestion but does not eliminate it. There are a few exceptions, such as Interstate 15 in San Diego, California, and an urban road in Singapore, where charges are adjusted continuously, depending on traffic conditions, to achieve free flow. But elsewhere, as in central London, fixed charges are levied for simplicity and predictability, charges that are not high enough to ensure free flow at times of peak demand because the economists calculate that this would be suboptimal. So while journey times are shorter, they are not predictable.

A further big disadvantage of road pricing is the need to impose it on all road users, and to enforce this by identifying those who don't pay and penalising them. The costs of operating a road pricing scheme takes up a good part of the revenues. In contrast, predictive navigation is optional. No one is compelled to buy the receiving device or pay for traffic information. Those who do so will be regular road users who can benefit most. It would be sensible for the highway operators to provide a basic information service free of charge over the Internet, to smooth peaks and improve system efficiency. Private sector operators could provide a subscription service for those willing to pay that recommended alternative routes to avoid congestion hotspots. Because the capacity of such alternatives is limited, the cost of the subscription should be adjusted to limit users to a manageable number.

Third dimension

A quite different way of avoiding traffic congestion is to travel over or under the congested roads. Road traffic congestion is a problem in two dimensions. Might we take advantage of space in the third dimension? Travelling in tunnels is acceptable, provided we keep moving. But tunnels are expensive to construct and prone to cost overruns. A breakthrough in tunnelling technology that reduced costs substantially would be desirable but seems not in prospect. Nevertheless, 26 miles of new tunnels are being constructed under London as part of Crossrail, the new east-west rail route, and plans for Crossrail 2, a northeast-southwest line, have been issued for consultation.

Some cities have constructed roads in tunnels. Part of the outer orbital road around Paris is one of the longest urban road tunnels in the world, and other sections of the network have been roofed over to reduce traffic impact and provide new public spaces. Oslo is relocating a main surface road underground to create new waterside surface space. A recent report commissioned by the Mayor recommended investigation of this approach in London, as well as the possibility of small scale 'flyunders' to divert traffic from the surface.

Travelling above the traffic by helicopter is another costly mode, and noisy too, so use tends to be very limited in most major cities. São Paulo in Brazil may have the world's most extensive helicopter service, with the first dedicated air traffic control system for urban flights. Helicopter use by the wealthy reflects severe traffic congestion, inadequate public transport, anxiety about street violence and desire for an expensive status symbol. A breakthrough in helicopter technology that eliminated noise would permit wider use, but this seems unlikely. In any event, successful cities have good rail-based public transport, on the surface or below, which caters for rich and poor alike—a less socially divisive outcome.

A further variant on the theme of using the third dimension is an idea for technology that goes back half a century but which only now is beginning to be implemented in a way that has the prospect of making a wide impact. The concept known as Personal Rapid Transit (PRT) involves small automated taxi-type vehicles operating on a network of purpose-built guideways. A pioneering example opened at Heathrow Airport in 2011, linking Terminal 5 to its business car park, substituting, for the usual shuttle bus, four-person 'pods' operating at up to 25 mph on tracks above existing roads. This uses the technology known as 'Ultra', invented by Martin Lowson while at Bristol University. Reliability has been high, and the economics look promising. While initially trialled at an airport, this novel technology is intended as a solution to urban congestion and has considerable potential in appropriate locations. A large scheme is under construction at Amritsar in northern India, to carry up to 100,000 visitors a day to the Sikh Golden Temple.

More traditional forms of travel that resemble PRT are the funiculars which operate up and down cliffs or very steep slopes; lifts, elevators and escalators which are mostly in buildings but can operate outside; and cable cars, standard equipment for ski resorts but useful in cities, such as that over the River Thames in London's Docklands which opened in 2012. While these have niche roles for daily travel, they offer attractive views and add to the quality of city experience.

Rail redux

The nineteenth century was the great age of the railways. The twentieth century was the heyday of the motorcar, during which the railways went into decline, when many small lines in Britain and most of the passenger routes in the US closed down. But there has been a revival of rail in recent years in continental Europe and in the UK, with renewal of rolling stock, upgrading of track, as well as new high-speed routes. Demand for rail travel has been buoyant, with passenger numbers in Britain doubling from a low point in the early 1990s, and trains very crowded at time of peak usage. What rail offers, in contrast to congested roads, is speedy and reliable travel, which is safe, secure and sustainable—since it uses electricity for motive power. Time on trains can be spent productively with portable digital devices. For medium distances, rail is more attractive than air travel. While planes travel much faster, the time taken to get to airports, and queuing within them, offsets the higher speed.

There are in practice two kinds of surface transport: rail systems where entry is controlled and which offer speedy and reliable travel to set destinations; and the road system, good for door-to-door travel but open to all, with the result that congestion at busy times make journey duration uncertain. In a world in which populations are rising and more people are moving to cities, rail has advantages that offer the prospect for a continuing revival in the twenty-first century. The railways need now to cultivate a further virtue: that of 'seamless travel'. For this, good interconnections are needed across the broad network, including urban metros, trams and tramtrains (which run on rail tracks in the suburbs and along streets in city centres). Also important are online timetables and real-time information about performance; coordination with linking bus routes; smartcard ticketing, such as London's Oyster that you swipe at the barrier, best if it works for all public transport modes over a wide area. In short, rail has good prospects in competition with road if it can offer a quality journey free from hassle.

Two other technologies should be included in the broad category 'rail' since they offer unimpeded travel. To PRT mentioned above, we can add BRT, Bus Rapid Transit. These look like buses but run, largely or entirely, on dedicated guideways. Such systems were pioneered in Latin America and are growing in popularity worldwide, in part on account of lower costs compared with rail. The sixteen mile guided busway in Cambridge, opened in 2011, is the longest in the world, with passenger numbers well in excess of expectation and half those travelling in from outside the city previously having used a car.

Cycling

One transport technology that uses the road system but is not much affected by congestion is the bicycle. We use our muscles to power ourselves much more efficiently when we cycle than when we walk. Rather remarkably, we manage to balance on two wheels after only a little practice. Cycling requires a highly coordinated interplay between balance, coordination, and rhythmic movement of the legs. Patients suffering from Parkinson's disease, a neurological condition which impairs walking, can often continue to ride a bicycle, suggesting that a distinct set of neural pathways are involved.

Fossil fuel energy is not needed to propel a bike although it is essential for constructing the machine, to fabricate materials and components. So the bicycle is an innovation of the era of fossil fuel use and is the cheapest technology available for going faster than walking pace. It was the first transport technology that allowed people regularly to venture beyond their locality. Geneticist Steve Jones has pointed out that if one's ancestors came from the same village they might well have been related, but this is much less likely of they were born far apart. In early nineteenthcentury Oxfordshire, the average distance of between birthplaces of marriage partners was less than ten miles; now it is more than fifty and in the US it is several hundred. As a consequence of this increasing mobility, the world's populations are beginning to merge genetically. Steve Jones suggests the most important event in recent human evolution was the invention of the bicycle.

Bicycles, once they become generally affordable, are popular for the new opportunities they make possible. Mass bicycle use is typically succeeded by general adoption of motorised two-wheelers as incomes rise, which in turn give way to the car. But bicycle use can revive in higher income countries on account of the health benefits of exercise that forms part of the daily routine, reliable journey times, low cost and that 'wind in the hair' feeling, particularly when coasting down a gentle incline. Such revival tends to be led by male professional types who see cycling as the new golf (the workers prefer a proper set of wheels in the form of a white van). This sends the signal that using a bike does not imply that you can't afford a car. Successful and attractive cities such as Amsterdam and Copenhagen have high levels of cycle use, with over a third of trips to work by bike. Cycling is a good option over short to medium distances in level urban areas because its speed is competitive with buses and cars in peak hour traffic, so there is no loss of access. Cycle journey times depend on the energy of the rider but are largely independent of traffic conditions. Generally, urban cycling competes with buses and rail over moderate distances, but in practice tends not to displace car use, so it can relieve crowding on public transport but does not reduce traffic congestion. For this reason, the cycling renaissance in North America has been limited to the centres of a few dozen cities, with minimal impact in the suburbs.

In Britain only around two per cent of people say their main mode of travel is the bicycle, low compared with almost 20 per cent in Denmark and over 25 per cent in the Netherlands. Cycling in London has been growing briskly, doubling over the past ten years. Already, there are more cyclists than cars crossing the main Thames bridges during peak periods. This growth has largely been driven by individual choice and promoted by the marketing of bikes, as well as by a tax advantage for employers who loan cycles to employees. Companies are also converting basement car parks into bike storage, complete with lockers and shower facilities. A symptom of the fashion for cycling is that new, good quality apartments in some of the inner suburbs have bike storage space but no car parking space or onroad entitlement to parking.

Growth of cycling in London has been aided by public schemes such as cycle hire and the 'cycle superhighways', which provide commuter cyclists with clearly marked, faster, more direct journeys into the city. However, these routes are largely blue-painted lanes on normal roads. To get a big increase in cycle use, continuous segregated cycle lanes would be needed to protect cyclists from faster traffic, particularly large lorries, and to expand the market beyond mainly intrepid younger men. In early 2013 the Mayor of London, a well-publicised cyclist himself, announced ambitious plans to expand cycling facilities, including a fifteen-mile east-west segregated route. This is a welcome development because cycling is a low cost mode of travel, both for the rider and public authorities responsible for infrastructure. Modest investment in cycle lanes will help defer substantial investment in public transport needed to cope with a growing population.

Motorcycles and scooters, like bicycles, have advantages in congested traffic. Numbers on British roads reached a peak in the 1960s, fell back subsequently as higher incomes allowed people to switch to cars, but have grown again in recent years, mainly as a lower cost alternative for commuting. Nevertheless, pushbikes are used for four times as many trips as motorised two wheelers. However, the distinction between the two is diminishing with the development of electric bicycles and electric traction for scooters. In Shanghai and Beijing silent electric scooters have largely or entirely replaced conventional engines, motivated by lower running costs and the need to reduce emissions.

Technology futures

Transport technologies evolve slowly. They are constrained by the weight of all the fabrications already in place, the interdependence on both the infrastructure and the supply chains that deliver energy to the sector, the slow turnover of the vehicle stock (typical lives: fifteen years for cars, twenty-five for planes), as well as safety imperatives—you can accept your computer 'crashing' from time to time, but not your car. Long time car makers such as Ford are still major players, having accumulated deep experience of vehicle and manufacturing technologies, and of the needs of their customers.

Existing transport technologies will incrementally improve and refine, and old technologies like the bicycle can be revived. In contrast, the digital technologies leap forward. However, the scale of their potential impact on travel is not yet apparent. The book you are reading is available as an e-book. The black type on a white page is not fundamentally different in appearance from the earliest hand-printed books of the fifteenth century or the output of the mechanised presses of the nineteenth. What is distinctive is digital distribution that cuts out the printer, bookshop and library, and allows you to buy this book for the price of a sandwich. This is good for authors and readers, but for printers, bookshops, libraries and publishers, the e-book is a 'disruptive innovation' that is undermining existing ways of doing business.

At present we have examples of digital technologies improving journeys with Satnav and smartcard ticketing, and of allowing travel substitution, as when we work at home with access to the full range of information and contacts that we would have in our workplace. But these are not radical innovations. Are there disruptive innovations on the horizon for the transport sector?

Consider the driverless cars that are being developed by some manufacturers as well as by Google. The technologies required have been worked on for some years and those already introduced include adaptive cruise control, lane detection, pedestrian recognition, emergency braking and automated parking assistance. Hands-free driving is the logical extension. This might help prolong use of the car by older people, and could offer enhanced safety for all. Technologies that forgive us our errors are always helpful, especially in later life, although there will be the need to settle tricky questions of responsibility for crashes. However, it is hard to see any radical change for road users generally, given continued unconstrained access to the road system. You might think it would be useful to send your driverless car travelling around the block while you go into a shop. But then the streets would be jammed with 'parked' cars on the move, which evidently could not be permitted.

A segregated highway would allow platoons of driverless cars to operate in synchrony, thus increasing the capacity of the road. There have been successful experimental trials of platooning, but both wide practical implementation and economic attractiveness seem problematic. This is an chicken-and-egg situation: investment in a segregated highway could only be justified if there were a sufficient number of autonomous vehicles wiling to pay tolls for use, but investment in these vehicles could only be justified if the segregated highway existed. My expectation is that driverless cars, to the extent they penetrate the market, will amount to an incremental improvement, not a disruptive innovation—best regarded as robot chauffeurs. One possible application of this technology would be to taxis, if lower fares increased their attraction to passengers (in which case the innovation would be disruptive to taxi drivers). Driverless trains are already with us—for instance on London's Docklands Light Railway—safe and practical because access to the system is controlled.

Clayton Christensen, originator of the concept of disruptive innovation, argued that the electric car might be such a technology. Possibly the electric car will displace vehicles powered by conventional internal combustion engines. Car manufacturers who do not have access to this technology would lose market share, but the battery manufacturers who might make the technological breakthrough would be keen to supply all users. However, from the viewpoint of drivers and those responsible for the road system, changing the power source is an incremental improvement, not a disruptive innovation (although electric vehicles would be disruptive for the oil industry).

The key question for this chapter is whether advances in technology will allow us to travel significantly faster or very differently, whether through innovations that lead to new kinds of vehicle or new digital applications that provide trip information. In my judgement, the answer is probably not. While there will continue to be incremental improvements, the future of the car and of the other transport technologies is likely to be rather unexciting. This this does not matter, however, because we get most of what we need from travel at current speeds.

Chapter Six:

Decisions, Decisions

In the developed economies, travel and transport take a big chunk of a family's budget, second only to housing. There are trade-offs between the two. For many, lower house prices are possible by making a longer, more costly commute. For others, a longer commute allows income to be spent buying a larger house in pleasant surroundings. Decisions about where to live and how to travel are interrelated. But these personal decisions also depend on public decisions since the need for a car, or a second car, can depend on how good is the local public transport or how safe are the roads for cycling.

One of the big lifetime decisions is to buy the first car. The first outing is exciting. It feels liberating. Personal decisions about travel depend on feelings as well as on the practicalities of getting from A to B. The kind of car we want depends on how we see ourselves—thrusting and dynamic or relaxed and practical. But we might feel that we don't want to be car dependent, emitting greenhouse gases and noxious pollutants, playing our part in concreting over the countryside. So more of us are getting on our bikes.

Political culture is important. In the United States, the emphasis on individual freedom and the wide-open spaces of the historic frontier are the context for the largest vehicles and highest levels of ownership and use, as well as relatively low gasoline taxes—and therefore fairly limited public transport. Tightly packed European cities have long depended on buses, trams, metros and suburban trains for mobility, while cars are smaller and more economical on account of high fuel taxes.

Personal decisions on travel are intertwined with public

decisions taken through the political process, as well as business decisions taken by firms providing transport. So our options for a short break in the sun depend on what we can afford, what routes the private sector airlines have chosen to fly, and what airport capacity public authorities have been willing to permit. Investing in transport infrastructure has been an important way for governments to foster economic growth in a lagging region. But when capacity is stretched and the local environmental impact is large, as at London's Heathrow airport, then an option for governments is to call a halt in response to the anxieties of the local inhabitants about environmental damage.

Tools for decision makers

To bring discipline to public decisions on transport investment, the economists have developed the tool of 'cost-benefit analysis'. The idea is to put monetary values to the cost of building a new road, say, and compare this with the benefits. The main benefit is supposed to be the saving of time, since travel on the new road is faster than on the old. This time-saving is valuable, the transport economists argue, because it is time that could now be used for more useful activities, whether work or leisure. Having estimated the costs and benefits of the possible investments that might be made, the economists would want schemes with the highest ratio of benefits to costs to be given the highest priority, because that makes the best use of public resources. The politicians in transport ministries listen to what the economists propose, take this into account to varying degrees, and then make decisions that they think they can best justify to the voters.

One problem with cost-benefit analysis is that some important impacts are hard to value in money terms—damage from inserting a new road into an unspoilt landscape, for instance. Efforts have been made to value environmental, social and health impacts of new transport infrastructure and operations—with some success but still leaving significant gaps in our understanding.

In many areas of public expenditure the benefits are hard to value in terms of money, for instance of new hospitals and schools to replace obsolete buildings, or of prisons and military facilities where the aim is to enhance security. In these situations, 'cost-effectiveness analysis' is employed, rather than cost-benefit analysis. This involves estimating the costs of options for achieving some desired outcome, for example a new hospital in place of a nineteenth century building, to aid decisions in which expenditure is an important consideration. The transport sector, however, has resolutely adhered to cost=benefit analysis as the economists' 'gold standard', and has developed it in excruciating detail, despite a glaring anomaly.

The anomaly or discrepancy associated with conventional transport cost benefit analysis is that average travel time has held steady over the years at about an hour a day, as I explained in Chapter 1. This means that supposed travel time savings are transient, short run. In the long run, people take advantage of faster travel to go further, to gain access to a wider range of destinations and have more choices and opportunities. This increased access leads to changes in how land is used, most obviously as property development in the form of new homes and new commercial premises, both retail and workspace. Less visibly, upgrading of existing properties is important, such as gentrification of low cost housing made more accessible to employment opportunities by a new transport service Faster travel allows people to have more choices of homes, jobs, shopping, education and the rest.

Transport infrastructure and the buildings it makes accessible generally last a very long time. So short run travel time-savings are not a sound basis for valuing the benefits of better transport. We must identify and value the long-run economic benefits, which show up in the first instance as increased land and property values, and as new developments; and subsequently as new employment opportunities and more homes.

The transport economists have not yet caught up with one of the more important developments in economics in recent decades—'behavioural economics'—which arose from the observation of a series of discrepancies between how economic theory predicts rational decision-makers would act in their own best interests, and how people do in fact act in the real world. The message of behavioural economics, which has gained considerable traction amongst policy makers, is that if we are to influence behaviour to achieve better outcomes then we must base interventions on observations of what people actually do, rather than suppositions what they *might* do because the latter is easier to model. Travel time-savings are easier to model than the improvements in access and the consequential land use changes. Timesavings are estimated for convenience, even though this does not reflect the real changes in behaviour as a result of investment. This is the anomaly of conventional transport economics. The upshot has been poorly targeted expenditure, for instance the large sums to widen congested motorways, which then quickly fill up with traffic (discussed in Chapter 5).

Rail investment

Transport investment can be highly effective, in the right time and place. The railway construction of the nineteenth century transformed the landscape and was crucial for economic development, even though excessive enthusiasm created a boom in which investors overreached themselves and many lost money. The programmes of inter-urban road construction of the twentieth century have also been transformational—the autobahns in Germany, the Interstate Highway System in the US, the British motorways. But the developed economies now have largely mature transport networks and the case for further investment is less obvious. (There remain extensive opportunities for transport investment in the developing economies, of course.)

One type of transport investment that is of increasing importance is in railways. Rail travel is booming in Britain and growing in many other European countries. This is partly the consequence of investment on the supply side in the form of modern rolling stock, track upgrading and electrification. These improvements attract passengers out of their cars with the offer of speedy, reliable and comfortable travel away from congested roads. Demand for rail travel is also rising because car ownership and use have peaked in London and other cities, as explained in Chapter 2. Londoners without cars naturally turn to rail for medium-distance trips beyond the city, as do many Londoners with cars who have become used to rail for the journey to work.

High-speed rail is now common in Europe. Britain rather lagged, in part because the inter-urban distances tend to be shorter, which meant the benefit of higher speed is proportionately less. The first route, now known as HS1, connects the Channel Tunnel with London and permits travel to Paris in only 2½ hours. This has been a technical success although passenger demand proved substantially less than forecast and as a result, the company formed to construct the route got into financial difficulties and had to be bailed out by the UK government.

The British government has announced plans to build a second highspeed rail route (HS2) north from London, connecting to the main cities of the Midlands and North of England. While supported by the main political parties as necessary to increase capacity to meet rising demand, the project is strongly resisted by those whose properties would be adversely affected by the new track that has to cross unspoilt countryside. For those so affected, there is not even the consolation of a nearby station to take advantage of the new route since the benefits of high speed are reduced by stopping at intermediate stations. HS2 is intended to travel non-stop between London and Birmingham, the second city of Britain, reducing the travel time from 1 hour 25 minutes to 50 minutes.

Building a new railway from scratch is expensive. Critics of HS2 query whether it would amount to good value for money for the taxpayer who will have to fund the capital cost, and point to the loss of opportunity to invest elsewhere, for instance in urban and inter-urban rail schemes outside London which could boost local economies. The conventional estimate, based on the saving of travel time, yields benefits worth about twice the expected costs, implying a benefit-to-cost ratio of 2, a figure likely to be subject to revision as both estimates of costs and benefits are refined. There continues to be debate about the value of time-savings for people travelling on business. Critics point out that a lot of work gets done while people travel by train, particularly with mobile technology, and business travellers report that time spent working on trains is very worthwhile, which means the benefits of time saved can be overstated.

A further difficulty with the case for HS2 is that in general the long-run benefits from faster travel take the form of property development and upgrading, not time-saving. So the question is where will the development arising from HS2 arise. Consider Crossrail, another big rail project currently under construction across London. This is a new route that tunnels under central London, emerging to the surface on the east and west sides. In my view, it is fairly straightforward to predict the resulting land use changes, particularly west of London which has traditionally been more attractive for living than the east side of the city. Construction of Crossrail will save ten minutes crossing London from the west to the financial district in the east, which will allow ten minutes more commuting time from more distant, pleasant residential locations, both by longer distance rail and by car from outlying villages to stations on the route. There will be pressure to build new houses on land brought within commuting distance of central London, with big gains to land owners. Where the locals successfully resist new building, values of existing property will increase on account of greater demand from commuters.

Land value enhancement

An example where changes in land use are even more predictable is the scheme to develop the area in central London known as Nine Elms, which comprises extensive former industrial land along the river within a mile of the Houses of Parliament. The US Embassy is to relocate there, and there are plans for major residential and commercial developments. The area is to be made accessible by an extension of the Northern Line of the London Underground, a quarter the cost of which will be funded by means of contributions from the developers, which they are willing to make because the feasible scale of development would be much less without the access made possible by the Tube extension. More funding will be contributed by earmarking the higher business property taxes that are anticipated.

The Nine Elms case illustrates the need for public investment in transport to make an area accessible, so enabling private investment in residential and commercial property that creates employment and homes. It also illustrates the willingness of developers to part fund transport infrastructure when this can unlock valuable land. The conventional methodology of the transport economists—which focuses on the supposed saving in travel time as the main benefit of investment—is not relevant. Such time-savings are notional, not observable. In contrast the property development and enhancement of value is real and observable. Indeed, prices of existing property often rise on the announcement of a transport improvement, as prospective purchasers anticipate the benefit of the improved access. Yet the economists neglect these consequences—mistakenly, in my view.

One reason why the transport economists prefer to disregard land use changes is that these are often not firmly predictable since they depend on planning decisions by local authorities in response to proposals from developers, which may take time to come forward. While the land use consequences are clearly foreseeable for Nine Elms, and for Crossrail reasonably so, they are far less certain for HS2. The big question is the scale of benefits for the cities outside London, in Birmingham, Manchester, Leeds and beyond. Britain has always been dominated by London politically. Economically, this dominance has tended to increase as manufacturing has declined in importance and the service sector has grown. London once had a substantial manufacturing sector—clothing, furniture, consumer goods—but this has largely been replaced by services, not just finance but also other business services such as accountancy, legal, consultancy, design, creative and media. The regions outside London seek government support for developing economic activity to replace declining traditional sectors, and would like to see HS2 as helpful to this end. The risk is that the new rail route could end up by benefitting London more, by reducing the need for businesses based in the capital to have regional presences.

There was a news item in the Financial Times in 2010 reporting a tendency for firms with factories in the Midlands and the North to relocate their head offices to London, both to facilitate business with international clients and to improve access to a pool of suitable non-executive directors. This was newsworthy because of the concern that such a trend might weaken the regions. What impact might HS2 have on this tendency? Would it facilitate the movement of head offices to London, because staff from the factories could more easily travel to meet senior management? Or would it reverse the trend, as international clients and non-executives enjoyed the experience of travel by high-speed rail? We cannot answer this question with any confidence. The experience of the local impact of highspeed rail in Europe and elsewhere is decidedly mixed.

Regeneration

What has been happening in London's former Docklands illustrate the range of development outcomes possible from rail investment. The Docklands Light Railway (DLR) was envisaged as a means for regenerating the area, once shipping had moved down river to berths suited to large container vessels. It was expected that low-cost office accommodation would allow back office staff to be moved out of high rent space in the City, the historic financial centre. The first phase of the DLR showed how accessible was Canary Wharf, the nearest part of the former docks, from the City, and prompted developers to construct new high rise, high value accommodation suitable for international and European head offices of the major financial firms. Most of the rest of Docklands has been developed as lower rise, lower value business accommodation. We also find there London's largest exhibition centre and entertainment venue, a popular small airport for business travel, the 2012 Olympics park and sports facilities, expanding universities, a large shopping complex, and extensive new apartment buildings to house London's growing population.

East London is undergoing regeneration based on investment in rail lines, as I discussed in Chapter 3. Public investment in speedy and reliable rail transport has made possible private investment in residential and commercial property development. This is how the economic benefit of public investment is works through. It was never possible to justify investment in the DLR or the extension of the Jubilee Line on the basis of travel time-savings, partly because few people travelled to the area before regeneration. But the commitment to phase 1 of the DLR was undoubtedly a farsighted and bold decision that illustrates well the case for seeking transformational change from such strategic transport investment.

So what of HS2? Can we expect transformational change to the cities that will be connected by it to the capital? It's hard to say, not just because of mixed experience in Europe, but also because the development of the necessary analytical tools has been neglected. Because the transport economists (and the Department for Transport following their advice) are so fixated on time-savings as the benefit of investment, they have failed to develop models that relate transport improvements to changes in land use. Conventional transport modelling focuses on changes in travel behaviour assuming land use remains unaltered. What is needed are models which recognise that average travel time holds constant in the long run, and that what changes is land use. If we had developed, calibrated and validated such models, we would be better placed to assess the potentially transformational benefits of projects such as HS2.

In practice, if HS2 is to be built, the question for the regional cities becomes how to get the most out of it. They can offer accommodation costs lower than London, and so may be able to attract staff away from the capital. Businesses that maintain offices in both London and the main provincial cities might move some staff away from the head office, both for lower office rents and more affordable housing for staff. To gain this business, the cities will need to permit office development adjacent to the new stations. The other approach open to the regional cities is to focus on activities that are not carried out in London. Birmingham arose to prominence as a centre of manufacturing in the eighteenth century, with an innovative, entrepreneurial culture. Although service activity now dominates the local economy, revival of specialist manufacturing would allow Birmingham to complement London, rather than compete.

There is a long running debate about how best to foster economic development in Britain outside London and southeast England to which activity seems naturally to flow. The cities of the Midlands and the North that will be served by HS2 see the new route as likely to help their revival (although nearby towns not on the route are anxious about losing business if the impact is to redistribute economic activity rather than generate it). London views the new service as meeting the needs of its inhabitants for speedy travel northwards. These different but complementary perspectives create political impetus, despite the high cost. At this stage it is hard to judge whether everyone will get prizes.

More generally, plans for new investment in the railway will help meet the travel needs of a growing population living in existing urban centres. But people buying new homes on greenfield sites on the edge of existing towns and cities will want cars to get around. There may be a need for more local road capacity, although there is little public appetite in Britain for any major road construction. Public expenditure on roads is targeted on sweating the existing assets plus incremental improvements at bottlenecks in the system. The hard shoulders of existing motorways, intended for emergency use when cars broke down more often than they do now, are being converted to vehicles lanes at times of peak demand. The civil engineering work involved is expensive and yields limited real benefit. The aim is to improve the performance of the strategic road network, but most of the benefit is taken by local traffic, not long distance traffic—the standard appraisal method does not recognise this important distinction. I noted in the last chapter that an evaluation of 58 major road schemes implemented by the Highways Agency (responsible for England's motorways and trunk roads) found time-savings to road users at peak times of only three minutes on average. If, as I expect, these benefits show up in the long run as changes in land use, they will be quite modest and spread thinly across the country—little you could observe in practice. We would do better to take advantage of digital technologies to cope with congestion, rather than make futile attempts to build our way out of it, as I argued in Chapter 5.

The UK trunk road system is mature. The era of major road construction has ended. The big debate about transport infrastructure investment focuses on railways, and on runway capacity at airports in southeast England, as discussed in Chapter 4.

Subsidies

The main subject of this chapter is how we make decisions about public investment in new transport facilities, whether roads or railways. In the UK and many other developed countries there is a belief held by economists and civil servants in thorough cost-benefit analysis as an aid to good decision making. But there is another kind of public expenditure on the transport system that escapes such scrutiny. This is the subsidy of operations, for which no proper economic appraisal is conducted. Subsidy may be substantial. For instance, at times in recent years taxpayers have contributed as much to the running of Britain's railways as have passengers' fares. Governments may aim to reduce such costly subsidy by seeking efficiency improvements and raising fares faster than the rate of inflation.

Commuters, who have made decisions about where to live based on house prices, the neighbourhood and the cost of annual travel, naturally resist rising fares, which both reduce their other expenditures and have an adverse impact on house prices as the attractions of longer distance commuting are lessened. Higher fares do not change travel time, so conventional cost-benefit analysis does not illuminate decisions on subsidies. However, a focus on land use changes, including changes in property values, would make cost-benefit analysis relevant.

Expenditure in Britain on all forms of transport has remained at about fifteen per cent of total household expenditure on average for many years. This is at the top end of the range for developed countries, reflecting our relatively high level of tax on motor fuels and low level of subsidy of public transport. People often grumble about high fares in comparison with other countries they visit. But reducing fares would mean higher taxes, which would not be welcome. There is room for improvement in operational efficiency on the railways, however, which could help contain future increases in fares.

The scale of subsidy affects fares and hence use of the railways, which in turn affects crowding at peak times. Investment to reduce crowding, for instance in longer trains and platforms, is clearly beneficial but does not offer travel time-savings and so gets only modest recognition in conventional appraisal. But increasing capacity does allow more people to travel, therefore increasing property use and values at both ends of the trip—which are economic benefits that should to be taken into account.

Subsidy that reduces fares encourages more use of the railway and thus less use of the car, which is helpful for reducing both carbon emissions and congestion. It also lessens the need to invest in the road network. Public expenditure on the transport system takes two forms, capital investment and operational subsidy. Decisions on the scale and balance of these need a strategic vision.

Big decisions

The UK is planning a major increase in public investment on the transport system in the coming years: £50bn for HS2, £16bn for other rail expenditure over the five years from 2014, and £30-50bn on major road projects over ten to fifteen years. There is also likely to be substantial expenditure on airports, although it is uncertain where this might take place and how it may be split between public and private sector funders. For all this investment, the problem facing us is the lack of clarity about the benefits from such huge public expenditure, which pre-empts other kinds of worthwhile investment, whether in the transport sector—urban metros in provincial cities, for instance—or elsewhere. Lack of clarity about the benefits of investment precludes any kind of strategic vision for the future development of the transport system.

Cost-benefit analysis as currently practiced, with its focus on supposed time-savings as the main economic benefit, is misleading because it does not reflect the way in which people in fact take the benefits of investment. It overstates the benefits of incremental road investment; finds it difficult to take account of the value of reliability and hence the case for investment in digital technologies that reduce journey time uncertainty; and understates the benefits of transformative rail investment. So applying cost-benefit analysis leads to poor investment decisions, which is an important reason why transport policy in Britain has been ineffectual in recent years.

Ignoring changes in land use is a fatal flaw, in particular the disregard of development of new homes and workplaces. We need to recognise the economic consequences of land use changes brought about by better transport in an improved cost-benefit methodology. Or we might simplify decision-making by deciding what we want to achieve and using cost-effectiveness analysis to get best value for money.

More generally, thc aspiration of the transport economists to link investment to the theoretical increase in value to society (termed 'welfare benefits') has resulted in a disconnect with real, observable benefits to the economy that increase national wealth. The standard approaches to investment appraisal and transport modelling do not illuminate the real world economic benefits for which we hope.

A further problem is the uncertainty of future travel demand. The central theme of this book is the growth of travel per person, including car travel, in the developed economies has now levelled off. However, official forecasters, including those in the UK Department for Transport, do not yet recognise this and so project growing per capita demand. For instance, the latest car traffic forecasts for Britain project an increase by 2040 of over 40 per cent while population growth is expected to be around 20 per cent. Such predicted traffic growth provides a justification for large investment in the road network, growth which, in the event, might either not arise or might only arise because additional road capacity is created—the 'induced traffic' phenomenon discussed in Chapter 5. Either way, the economic benefits remain unclear.

Bent Flyvjberg, an economic geographer, has studied major infrastructure projects ('megaprojects') and why they fail. He finds that costs frequently tend to be higher than forecast and demand lower, which he attributes to a combination of psychological factors, particularly 'delusional optimism' of managers, and political explanations whereby promoters intentionally overstate demand and understate costs in order to increase the likelihood that their projects get funded, rather than those of competitors—known as 'strategic misrepresentation'. These shortcomings could also apply to programmes of public investment such as the UK's new roads programme.

My experience when a member of the British civil service is that high quality, unbiased policy and economic analysis is the aspiration of all those involved and can be achieved if carried out in advance, to inform policy decisions. But if the policy is settled first, then the analysts are torn between doing a good professional job and meeting the needs of ministers for an economic analysis that supports the decision taken. Politicians like to offer hope, and expect evidence to support their proposals. This is the situation for HS2 as well as for the new UK programme of roads investment, both of which enthuse ministers in expectation of stimulus to the wider economy. More generally, any ministry of transport will tend to protect its budget against cuts sought by its finance ministry by playing up travel demand forecasts and investment benefits and playing down project costs. It is then hard for a transport ministry to revise downwards forecasts of future demand in advance of that being forced by the actual outcome.

Businesses in the private sector need to be realistic when projecting future demand since they bear the cost of over-optimistic forecasts. As a salutatory example, passenger numbers on HS1, the high-speed railway linking London to the Channel Tunnel, turned out to be only a third of the original forecasts of the private sector operator because competition from the low-cost airlines and the ferries had been underestimated. The operator became insolvent, the investors lost their money and the route had to be bailed out by the Department for Transport, which in turn made over-optimistic forecasts of demand. The threat of insolvency bears much more heavily on private sector entities than on those in the public sector. This is why the car manufacturers seem more realistic about the way demand for their products is changing than are the transport ministries.

The British government recently set up an Office for Budget Responsibility (OBR) to provide independent, authoritative analysis and forecasts of the UK's public finances. There would be much to be said for a similar body to oversee the major public investment programmes, to advise whether value for money is likely to be attained, and whether the government's wider objectives are likely to be met. Indeed, given the importance attached to such investment for the future of the economy, there is a good argument for extending the remit of the OBR to provide dispassionate analysis of demand forecasts, costs and benefits of all major publicly funded infrastructure schemes.

Chapter Seven:

Travellers' Tales

Travel has always been more than about getting from A to B, from home to work, from one place to another. Daily travel gets us out of doors, engaging with our neighbours and the wider world, exercise from walking and cycling, the sense of movement. Much recreation involves moving through the landscape, sometimes slowly as when hiking or sailing. Going faster adds pleasure—the feel of wind through the hair—for those who have the ability: jogging, running, cycling, horse riding, motor biking, skiing, boarding on snow, surf or concrete. Even two-year olds gleefully speed on their three-wheel mini-scooters, later using this not insignificant transport innovation to go happily to school, saving parents from dragging or driving their unwilling offspring. From our hunter-gatherer ancestors we have inherited a deep impetus to be mobile, as well as a physiology adapted to regular exercise. We do well to cultivate this inheritance or else experience sluggishness of mind and body, with obesity, cardiovascular disease and dementia more likely to ensue. The onset of frailty in later life can be postponed through exercise, of which the most basic form is walking.

I reported in Chapter 1 that for any population, average travel time is about an hour a day. Why so? Evidently there has to be some upper limit to the amount of time we spend on the move. There are only 24 hours in the day and we must eat, work, sleep, socialise and the rest. But why have we not taken advantage of faster travel to spend less time travelling, as the economists suppose we should? One reason, I suggest, is that our genetic and cultural inheritance prompts us to be mobile, to get out of the house, stretch our legs and see the world.

Mobility and narrative

Famine or chronic hunger was not uncommon before modern times. Early hominids that moved on to find new hunting grounds would have had greater reproductive success than those who were less adventurous. A predisposition to explore would be advantageous in times of scarcity or danger—to climb to mountaintops to see what is beyond or to brave the dark woods. Such a predilection for mobility seems a universal feature of the human condition as variously manifested: the daily need to get out of the house; the attraction of the long adventurous trip, whether gap year travel, ocean sailing, or the trek through wild places; and historic migration to all the habitable parts of the earth.

Longer distance travel involves adventure, even today. We get satisfaction from overcoming inconvenience and discomfort to attain the summit for the panoramic view; or, more modestly, from reaching our holiday beach; or, more heroically, as migrants arriving at our journey's end. Yet for much long distance travel, it is less the destination that matters, more the sense of moving on and of what is encountered en route. Robert Louis Stevenson, traveller and author of adventure stories, captured this feeling: 'For my part, I travel not to go anywhere, but to go. I travel for travel's sake. The great affair is to move.'

But without the trouble and expense of travelling, we can experience vicariously, as armchair travellers, some of the adventurer's experience via the extraordinarily popular genre of 'travel writing'. This has deep roots, going back to the biblical stories of the Exodus of the Israelites from Egypt, and the Odyssey, the long journey home of Odysseus after the fall of Troy. Most cultures have such ancient epic tales: of exile, migration, invasion, discovery, escape, quest, pilgrimage—travel as an ordeal, a challenge, experience to be endured, suffering which transforms. The hearers of these narratives, who rarely left the villages of their birth, were surely entranced by the stories passed down orally by poets and singers, as well as by the more common tales of returning travellers.

Narrative is a universal feature of human cultures. We are surrounded by stories—in books, films, plays, newspapers and magazines. Libraries are full of stories. We all love to hear stories and many are keen to tell them, whether anecdotes for friends, blogs of our travels or, more ambitiously, as published fiction and memoir. Stories can be fictional or factual. Discoveries made by scientists involve telling a story about causes and effects, how observable phenomena are linked together. This book is a story. It seems that as our brains evolved, we developed a mind module that creates narratives from what we observe and imagine. Such narratives would have been advantageous in capturing and passing on the experience of explorers who travelled beyond the bounds of their community, so preserving the knowledge gained which might be crucial for survival in times of stress or danger. The oral literature of surviving forager societies is found to concern itself particularly with the lay of the land, travel routes, and orienteering—knowledge critical to undertaking extended hunting, trading, or visiting trips, which are an important part of forager life.

In short, the ubiquity of both mobility and narrative suggests that our species has succeeded through selection of two traits: a predisposition to explore beyond the territory presently inhabited; and an ability to capture the experience gained through telling and hearing stories. The common feature is the generation of a flow of useful new knowledge. A further conjecture is that poetry—rhyme, metre and alliteration—developed as a means of preserving the accuracy of stories handed down orally. An evolved satisfaction from composing and hearing poetry would serve a useful practical purpose before tales could be written down.

Travel writing

Writing, and later printing, allowed travellers stories to be widely disseminated. Marco Polo's account of his journey through Asia in the thirteenth century is the bestknown early travel book. Since then the genre has blossomed, reflecting the need of the readers for factual stories, both for their own sake, allowing us some sense of the experience without all the trouble, but also to suggest possible trips that we might make ourselves. In the twentieth century, travel writing developed considerably, based on the insight that the writer must undergo some form of personal transformation otherwise their experience and writing would be merely formulaic, akin to a guidebook.

Paul Fussell, in his account of British travel writing between the two world wars, argued that the 1920s and 1930s were the 'final age of travel'. The latter half of the twentieth century, with its cheap air travel, permitted mass tourism. Before tourism there was 'travel', and before travel there was exploration and pilgrimage. Travel involves work, risk, uncertainty and discomfort, with the worst trips making the best reading. Tourism, on the other hand, gets us out and back with minimal surprise and discomfort, ideally. We return with our individual narratives, extensively illustrated with digital photographs. Nevertheless, we still enjoy those personal, reflective accounts of the best contemporary travel writers, such as Bruce Chatwin, Jonathan Raban, Paul Theroux and Colin Thubron, not least because they seem able to meet more interesting people on their travels than most of us can manage.

Even if classical travel writing is nowadays constrained by the possibility of tourists reaching the same places as the intrepid author, technology developments in the second half of the twentieth century permitted the return of travellers with their tales in the form of documentary film and video, particularly of rare animal, bird and fish species in hard-to-reach habitats. While we tourists might go whale-watching and, if lucky, catch a fleeting sight of perhaps a minke whale or a basking shark, we know that David Attenborough, to mention only the best-known television naturalist, will bring us awesome images of creatures that we could never glimpse.

So we can enlarge our experience of the world in which we live from our armchair, through books, television and video. To what extent does this substitute for actual long distance trips? For those who are too frail, too poor or even too nervous to travel, the armchair experience is a boon. But for the rest of us, I suspect the books and images act as a stimulus to travel, like the traditional brochures from the holiday agents. The countervailing influence is the actual experience of being a tourist in popular destinations—the sense that the originally charming and picturesque location has become a kind of theme park for our entertainment. For myself, I prefer to travel to relatively remote places where the weather is cool and unreliable, conscious that much of the attraction for me depends on a lack of popular appeal.

We humans have populated the habitable parts of our planet from the Equator to the Polar Regions and have thoroughly explored the uninhabited remainder. While there remain animal and plant species in remote corners yet to be discovered, we are at the end of the epoch of global exploration. Other planets beckon, but we would need technologies that allow us to travel much faster if the dream of human exploration of space is to become a reality.

We need to travel—it's in our genes and our culture. Mobility is a fundamental characteristic of humans and other animals, unlike plants, which are rooted. Our brains make intentional movement possible and thrive on the stimuli generated as we progress through the environment. The economists are concerned only with travel for the purpose of getting to a destination, not with the value of the experience of the journey. They see the saving of travel time as a benefit. In reality it is also a loss of experience. This is why on average we maintain our travelling time at about an hour a day—to avoid that loss.

Chapter Eight:

Fourth Era Travel

Looking back at human history, we see three eras of human mobility. First there were our hunter-gatherer ancestors, spending some of their time on the move foraging for food, some of the time sitting around socializing, travelling a few thousand miles a year on average. Second, our forebears settled in agricultural communities, worked harder to boost food production, with travel limited to about an hour a day and the distance walked amounting to about one thousand miles a year. Third, beginning two centuries ago, the modern era of mechanized transport that allows us to travel faster than on foot, taking advantage of the energy stored in fossil fuels. Time remains a constraint on travel, with the generally observed average of an hour a day reflecting the unchanging twenty-four hour day, the other necessary activities that must be fitted in, as well as our need to get out and about. The car very often achieves the highest door-to-door speeds for daily travel, road space permitting, and for this good reason has become the dominant mode of travel in the high-income countries.

We have now reached a time of transition, coming at the end of two centuries of growth of travel. Our lives have been transformed by our ability to use technology to travel faster. We have far more access to the kind of places we would like to reach, and far more choice of possibilities and opportunities for work, home, shopping, education, relationships and the rest. I have proposed that it is this high level of access, choice and opportunities that accounts for the cessation of growth of personal daily travel that is observed in developed countries.

A complementary influence is the difficulty of devising

technologies that would allow us to travel even faster at acceptable cost, safety and environmental impact. We seem to have reached the end of an era of technological advance. This is not unique to transport. Robert Gordon, a US economist, argues that there have been three industrial revolutions: the first created steam engines, cotton spinning and the railways; the second, electricity, the internal combustion engine and modern water supply. Both these required about one hundred years to percolate through the economy. The third, the computer and Internet revolution, began around 1960 and may have already had its main impact on productivity through displacing repetitive clerical work. There is no presumption that continued technological progress generally is inevitable. Particular improvements only happen once.

Demand saturation

Despite the constraints on going faster, we have enough daily travel to meet the needs of most of us who live in developed economies. Our demand for daily travel has saturated, as the economists and marketing people would put it. Demand saturation is what happens when ownership of a product reaches very high levels, so that market growth can only arise from population growth and sales are largely for replacement. Household ownership levels in developed economies commonly exceed 90 per cent for washing machines, microwave ovens, fridge freezers and the like, while mobile phone ownership exceeds one per person. Some household goods cease to grow at lower levels of ownership, for instance dishwashers at under 40 per cent in Britain, probably on account of small kitchens and the number of single person households. So we need not be surprised by the idea that daily travel demand has saturated.

Demand saturation is indeed advantageous in a world of resource constraints and an environment under stress. For the washing machine, we might aim to limit its impact by regulations that reduce energy and water consumption, foster robust construction to minimize maintenance and maximize useful life, and require recycling of materials when a machine is not longer usable. For motor vehicles, regulations for their construction and use take us increasingly in the same direction.

More generally, demand saturation is helpful for the idea of a low or zero growth economy, advocated by some economists outside the professional mainstream. Following the financial crisis that began in 2007, the developed economies are currently in a period of low growth that feels pretty uncomfortable. Because we have not planned for this, we must contend with the unintended and undesirable impacts such as cuts in public services and growing inequalities within society.

The domestic transport sector offers some helpful pointers as to how a low growth economy might function. There are plenty of breadwinner jobs that pay reasonably, in part because they are not subject to overseas competition or outsourcing (international transport is another matter). In Britain, 1.4 million people are employed in transport-related occupations and industries. The technologies change only slowly, so employment is fairly stable. When the private sector provides services, there is generally either sufficient competition or regulation to prevent excess profits at the expense of the travelling public. There are limited possibilities to pay more to travel faster, so 'first class' offers comfort, not higher speed. Transport is therefore a comparatively egalitarian domain, the main exceptions being in urban areas where rail is faster than bus travel, reflecting an acceptable trade-off between price and speed; and on uncongested roads where cars are quicker than using public transport, but where a top-of-the-range GT coupe, driven legally, is not much faster than a reasonably-priced family car. Transport economists generally favour road pricing as the response to congestion, but this does not appeal to the public, who prefer a shared experience of crowded roads. In short, the transport sector of the economy can cope with low or zero growth, which is in fact a feature of the fourth era of travel.

Demographics

While personal daily travel has reach a plateau, population growth continues. Demographic change now drives the increase in the total demand for travel. Where will the additional people live? If we build new houses on greenfield sites on the edge of existing towns and cities, then those who live there will want cars to get around these new suburbs. On the other hand, if growing populations are housed at higher densities in apartments within existing cities, then car use is limited by road capacity while public transport is increasingly viable.

London is an example of an economically dynamic, culturally vibrant, ethnically diverse city with a growing population that is being housed at increasing densities within the existing boundaries. London's road capacity has not increased, which constrains car use. Indeed, the allocation of carriageway for bus and cycles lanes, and for more pedestrian space, has further limited car use. As a result, car use in London, as measured by the number of daily trips or the amount of car traffic, has been flat for two decades. Because the population is growing, the share of trips by car is in decline, while the share for public transport is rising.

Peak car use occurred in London around 1990, when 50 per cent of all journeys were by car. This has now fallen to 38 per cent and I project car trips to decline further as the population continues to grow, to 30 per cent or less. The resulting increase in demand for public transport prompts new investment and improved services, which enhances its attractions. Moreover, declining car use and ownership in London has resulted in a substantial boost in demand for rail travel to towns and cities beyond.

Throughout the world, people are moving to cities. The urban population exceeds 70 per cent of the total in all regions except Asia and Africa, where the proportion is rapidly increasing. Globally, half the world's people live in towns and cities at present and this is expected to grow to approaching 70 per cent by mid-century. The combination of global population growth and increasing urbanisation means that urban numbers will double by midcentury. Expanding cities have a choice: whether to sprawl or to build to higher densities. Both possibilities have attractions. Many people, particularly families with children, like houses with gardens in pleasant suburbs. Others prefer the buzz of the busy city centre. Many cities are experiencing a central area revival after a period when it seemed that new service sector firms were moving out to isolated offices in edge-of-city business parks or to smaller towns further afield. But the tide turned. The desire of people and businesses to interact, both during working hours and after, is bringing them back to the city centre, which performs its traditional role as the place for mixing and matching, working and playing, cooperating and competing. Cities are where agglomeration spurs creativity, innovation, economic energy and cultural vitality.

Successful cities

For cities to function, their inhabitants have to be able to get around within them, and also to travel beyond. For low-density cities, the car dominates. But for high-density cities, there is too little road space for cars and buses, which become slow and unreliable ways of travelling due to traffic congestion. Successful cities are investing in speedy and reliable rail systems, whether above or below ground. Professionals and business people can be attracted out of their cars onto rail for the journey to work, but it's much harder to get them to use buses that travel no faster than their cars. We have, in effect, two classes of public transport in cities: fast and reliable at a premium price on rail; and slower, less reliable at a lower price by bus. Both are necessary and have their different customers.

Outside city centres, where there is space for cars to move and park, buses are mostly used by the young and the old. Two kinds of services are needed: daytime routes penetrating residential neighbourhoods for older people; and evening and weekend services running fast along main roads for younger people, who employ mobile technology and social media to know when the bus is coming, data for which is supplied by the operators and by the users themselves, crowdsourced. Effective use of digital technologies to monitor bus movements and to book rail travel online is a contributing factor to reduced interest by younger people in car ownership.

High-density cities allow more choices of facilities, of shops, cinemas, jobs and leisure. Catchment areas are smaller, whether for schools or supermarkets, making walking and cycling more feasible. Public transport has more customers so that services can be more frequent and new investment justified, creating a virtuous circle of demand growth and operational improvement. Denser cities are also suited for electric vehicles, both cars and delivery vans, since distances are shorter. Electric power for both road vehicles and urban rail helps reduce carbon emissions from the transport sector. Denser cities with declining car use and ownership stimulate demand for travel between cities by rail, further contributing to carbon reduction.

Many desirable residential areas in the world's wealthiest cities have high densities and building forms that minimize the need for space heating and cooling—much more so than housing in suburban or rural areas. Because rents and property prices are high, residents occupy less floor space and so incur lower energy costs. Cities also concentrate much of what contributes to a high quality of life that need not imply high material consumption levels—music, film, theatre, dance, visual arts, museums, colleges, libraries, the enjoyment of historic buildings and districts.

So we have the idea of the 'green metropolis'—cities where greenhouse gas emissions per person are substantially less than for suburban or rural lifestyles. Per inhabitant, London and Tokyo emit only about half the greenhouse gases of the average resident of Britain and Japan respectively. For New York City, Toronto and Rio de Janeiro, emissions per person are only 30 per cent of the national average.

While those of us who are mobile—whether by car, good public transport or bike—have plenty of choices, those lacking mobility are less fortunate. There is growing recognition of the importance of not excluding people with disabilities from participating in normal activities through barriers in the transport system and public spaces generally. Progress has been made in many countries in introducing new generations of buses and trains with good personal access. All London's buses are now accessible to wheelchairs.

Disability in later life is a prospect, or an actuality, for us all. For those dependent on the car for getting around, giving up driving can feel a big setback, particularly if you live in a rural area with little or no public transport. A better option is retirement to an urban neighbourhood with ready access to facilities without needing a car—a medium-density mature suburb, market town or seaside resort with good facilities served by buses. Free or cheaper travel on public transport for older people is popular and encourages them to give up the car.

The accommodation of a growing population, while minimising recourse to greenfield housing and car-based mobility, could be accomplished by some natural extension of higher density living across the lifespan. As an increasing proportion of the younger age groups attend universities and colleges that are now mainly on urban campuses, city centres are where students and recent graduates increasingly live, for job opportunities, part-time while at college and first-stage career afterwards, and for social involvement. The car is not part of this urban lifestyle. Having children and moving to the suburbs is increasingly delayed until a decade or so after graduation, putting off entry to family life, perhaps influenced by the prospects for this generation of living quite a bit longer than their parents. Later, when the children are grown and have flown the nest, there are attractions in a move to an urban environment that helps preserve independence through ready access to regularly used facilities and services.

Alternatives to Peak Car

Average total daily travel per person has stabilised in the *developed* economies and the future scale and pattern of the transport system that we shall need will depend on demographic factors—population growth, urbanisation, longevity and ageing. But for the still *developing* economies, there remains a big shortfall in mobility and access, the consequence of limited transport systems and low levels of car ownership. The populations of these countries naturally aspire to attaining the degree of access and choice that those in the developed world have achieved. But high car ownership in China, India and the other growing economies would have a sizeable global impact on oil demand and carbon emissions, as well as local impacts such as traffic congestion and air pollution. Is there a better route to high levels of access and choice than car-based mobility?

The experience of London, where we passed through a peak of car use and are now seeing a decline, suggests that an alternative path is available. The upper trajectory in Figure 3

Figure 3. Share of journeys by car

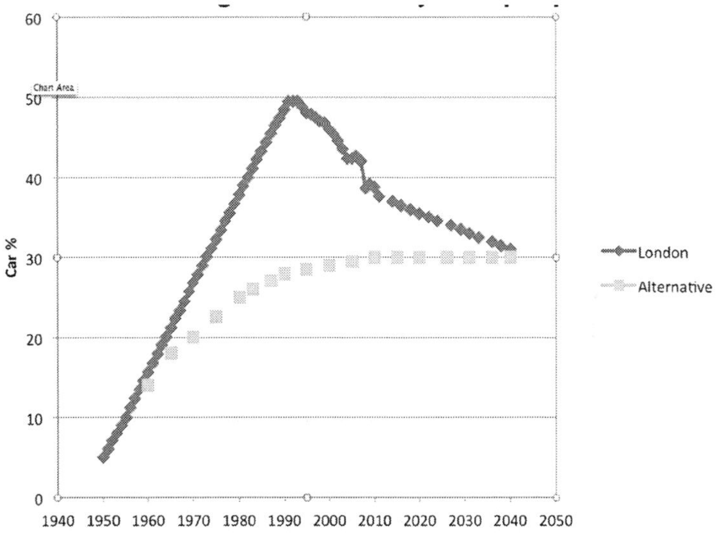

shows car use in London, expressed as the share of all journeys. The data for 1993 to the present are as estimated by Transport for London; the data prior to 1993 are my estimates, reflecting the growth of car ownership in Britain generally; and the extrapolation into the future is based on expected population growth, assuming no additional annual car trips are made because road capacity continues to be constrained. This Figure is the clearest manifestation of the 'peak car' phenomenon.

The lower trajectory in the Figure shows an alternative pathway that reaches the same outcome expected for London. For cities in developed countries, we are where we are and cannot now follow the path not taken. What historians would term the 'counterfactual' is of no more than theoretical interest. But for cities in developing countries still with low car ownership, there is the possibility of avoiding peak car, instead 'tunnelling under the peak', so to speak, lessening congestion, saving resources and reducing cumulative greenhouse gas and pollutant emissions. Whichever route taken, however, the 30 per cent of journeys by car projected when the population reaches ten million is quite low—less than half the share of trips currently made by car in Britain as a whole.

My proposition is that a medium density city of ten million inhabitants can be successful, economically and socially, if car trips are limited to around 30 percent of all journeys, based on current and anticipated experience in London. The main policy requirement to reach such an outcome would be to offer a rail alternative to road for work journeys, or, as a cheaper substitute, Bus Rapid Transit, which looks like a bus but behaves like a tram because it runs on dedicated road space. Speedy and reliable travel on a well-integrated public transport network allows a city to function.

To keep the roads sufficiently uncongested to allow buses, taxis, goods delivery and emergency vehicles to operate efficiently, car-parking needs to be controlled, particularly during working hours. Paying parking charges by mobile phone is common in developed cities and could be used in developing cities, given that nearly everyone who has a car also has a phone.

Bicycles are the dominant mode of urban travel when incomes are low, but are subsequently replaced first by motorised two-wheelers and then by cars. But cycling can be revived, by putting in place cycle lanes and low cost bike hire. Public cycle rental schemes are operating in more than 500 cities in 50 countries. The largest cycle hire scheme in the world is in the city of Hangzhou in south China. Cars will always be popular, but car sharing in its various forms is worth encouraging in preference to individual ownership, given that private cars are parked for

95 per cent of the time and that people who share cars drive substantially less those who own cars. Where politically feasible, as for instance in Singapore or Hong Kong, relatively high taxes on cars or on fuel can both raise revenue for investment in public transport and dampen the growth of ownership.

More than one billion motor vehicles populate the earth today. On one expert estimate, there could be two billion by as early as 2020, assuming continued rapid growth of ownership in the developing economies. But this may not be inevitable given urbanisation of populations, unavoidable constraints on car use in urban areas, and the possibilities for alternative modes of travel that allow cities like London to prosper.

Competing modes

In this fourth era of travel, four modes compete to meet our transport needs: road, rail, the slow modes, and air. We will use those that offer the best quality experience. A key distinction is between the road network open to all and the rail system where entry is controlled.

Because the road network is open to all vehicles, it tends to be congested in or near population centres at times of peak usage. Road pricing can be used to limit demand but is only feasible where an alternative is available for those deterred by the cost. This may be public transport in urban areas or the secondary road network elsewhere. The scope for reducing congestion by building more road space is limited by the tendency for road users to take advantage of the improvement to make longer journeys. Some shifting of demand away from times of peak usage is feasible by means of predictive traffic information that allows those with flexibility to adjust their travel plans. Travel by car will always be attractive beyond the inner suburbs of cities, but its popularity may be near its peak in developed economies.

Within cities, gridlock on the roads can be avoided through a combination of rail services for journeys to work, parking controls and other measures to constrain car use, together with sophisticated urban traffic management systems that continuously adjust timing of traffic signals to smooth flows and prioritise buses. London's ability to cope with a major shift in travel flows during the 2012 Olympic Games demonstrated the potential of comprehensive traffic management systems to keep the traffic moving, as well as the adaptability of the inhabitants. If essential time-critical journeys to work can be accommodated, people adjust the scheduling or destination of other trips, shopping for instance, to avoid excessive time spent in traffic. In a well-managed city, congestion tends to be self-limiting because travel time is limited. This is also true for a wellmanaged interurban road network.

Rail is not subject to traffic congestion, although route capacity is limited by safe operational headways, and carriages with uncontrolled entry can be uncomfortably overcrowded. There is scope for adding capacity by means of longer trains, better signalling and new track. The rail network as a whole can offer travel that is speedy, reliable, safe, secure, seamless, productive, and also sustainable, when, as is largely the case, electric traction is employed and when, in time, the electricity supply system is decarbonised. There are prospects for a considerable revival of rail travel, particularly in countries where there is an existing network that can be developed. Population growth and urbanisation result in larger, denser cities whose travel needs cannot be met by road transport. To be successful they must invest in rail-based transport. Increased urban rail use reduces the need for car ownership and use, resulting in increased demand for inter-urban rail travel.

Rail travel takes a number of forms, including standard heavy rail, various light rail types such as metros and trams, underground, overground, Bus Rapid Transit, as well as Personal Rapid Transit such as the 'pods' at Heathrow Airport, in effect driverless taxis on dedicated guideways. The need is to integrate all these forms of rail travel into a network that offers convenient journeys, with advice on optimal routes, real-time and predictive information, easy interchanges and swipe card ticketing. Integration between road and rail is harder in general, although the matching of bus and rail timetables to facilitate linked journeys is achievable. The point of integration is to achieve seamless journeys—less waiting, less queuing, less hassle, and more confidence about time of arrival.

The slow modes of walking and cycling are favoured in highdensity urban environments where catchment areas are smaller and distances to services shorter. A number of successful cities have high levels of cycling, which can be encouraged in other cities by cycle rental schemes and by constructing cycle lanes. Youth seems to be falling out of love with the clunky car, preferring mobile devices that fit in the pocket, and seeing virtue in cycling for getting around while enjoying both exercise and immersion in the urban environment. More cycling routes in cities will help those keen on fitness while relieving some of the pressure on public transport at peak times. Better environments for pedestrians encourage healthy walking. Improving the urban environment both attracts pedestrians and improves quality of life.

Travel demand saturation, as well as increased use of rail and the slow modes, is helpful as regards concerns about sustainability and carbon emissions. Aviation remains a worry in this respect, particularly given projections of substantial growth of demand and the concomitant needs for additional airport capacity. However, as for daily travel, time constrains travel by air, and for this reason it is possible that demand saturation by residents of developed economies is nearer than is generally supposed. As the developing economies grow richer, their emerging middle classes will want to travel abroad. Where will they go? The capacity of traditional historic tourist destinations is finite. The 2012 Olympics tested the ability of London to cope with an influx of visitors, which it managed in part because the usual tourists stayed away. As the historic destinations fill up, more beach resorts for mass tourism will be developed, as well as ever-larger cruise ships, which, when sailing slowly, emit less carbon per passenger than had they travelled by air.

Twenty-first century travel

The future pattern of travel will depend as much on factors outside the transport system as within it, in particular demographic developments and society's response to population growth and ageing. Public policy and investment can reinforce market developments that respond to the preference of many young adults for urban living without a car. Other variants of urban life may increasingly meet the needs of older adults who are getting to the point at which multiple minor disabilities incline them to give up driving. Transport policy needs to be seen as one element of the wider response to demographic, societal, economic and environmental developments.

The nineteenth century was the age of the railway, the twentieth century the heyday of the car. What of the twenty-first century? The railways are reviving so we go back to the future. What the rail system can offer is surface transport unimpeded by the car. Rail has potentially a persuasive offering if the industry can deliver. It will be aided by population growth and increasing density, which favours rail investment and disfavours the road system.

There have been two dominant global trends over the past two centuries: population growth and technological development. Population growth puts pressure on food and mineral resources and on the environment, not least through carbon emissions and their contribution to global warming. Transport accounts for a quarter of energy-related greenhouse gas emissions, and road vehicles are responsible for more than three-quarters of this. The tendency for people to move to the cities is helpful since inhabitants of dense urban areas occupy less space, use less energy, travel shorter distances and less by car than those in the suburbs. Urban density makes it easier to switch transport from oil to electricity and from individual to shared modes. While radical advances in transport technologies seem not in prospect, there is plenty of scope for valuable incremental progress, particularly in urban applications. The continuous improvement over many years to the performance, quality, reliability and comfort of cars exemplifies what can be done.

Good governance is crucial for responding to these developments. London has a Mayor with responsibilities for transport, planning, development, housing, economic development and regeneration, culture, health inequalities, and a number of environmental issues. This wide range of responsibilities, of which transport is probably the most important, fosters coherent transport planning and provision, in particular the ability to plan strategically for population growth. Around the world, strong mayors with visions for the future of their cities give high priority to the improvement of their transport systems, for good reason.

London also has an effective executive body in the form of Transport for London, responsible for both public transport and the main road network, which it is able to operate an integrated transport system and to invest to meet future travel demand. Other British cities are only beginning plan for their regions and have to contend with multiple local authorities, limited powers and competing private sector transport providers, all of which makes it more difficult to develop attractive alternatives to the car. Nationally, there is no joined-up thinking within government of how to accommodate a growing population through interlinked policies and investment for housing, employment and transport. Meanwhile transport policy operates within its own silo, separate from the other crucial policy functions, so that investment achieves less than it should.

It is easy to propose changes to the machinery of government, arguably a temptation best resisted. Nevertheless, the responsibilities of departments are in fact readjusted from time to time, which prompts me to suggest the creation of a Department of Planning and Transport, bringing land use policy and transport policy together so that the former provides the context for the latter. Such a department would take the lead on the response to population growth—the most recent projection for England being a substantial 8.6 per cent increase between 2011 and 2021.

A great diversity of policy and practice is found across countries. Cities can learn from the successes of others, both governance as well as practicalities such as urban street design, rerouting urban arterial roads into tunnels, cycle routes, Bus Rapid Transit, urban goods distribution schemes and many other innovative approaches. Each city has its own individual characteristics and will need to formulate its vision of what kind of a place it wants to be and how to get there. But a common question is how to accommodate the car. For the centres of large, growing cities, the car is of declining importance. Elsewhere, there are more choices for the citizens, although generally there is a trade-off between the convenience of the car for personal mobility and the impact of streams of cars, moving and parked, on the quality of urban existence and the economic dynamism generated by people in proximity. The success of individual cities and towns depends importantly on decisions involving this trade-off. The danger is that efforts to accommodate the car undermine the social interactions that contribute to the success of the city.

Cities have always been the places where innovation occurs. London is a suggestive model for the innovative city, attracting people who are willing to dispense with the personal car. Car use in London is well past its peak, as a proportion of all journeys. For entrepreneurs and creative people, the car seems to be increasingly yesterday's technology. 'The future is already here—it's just not evenly distributed.' said William Gibson, the science fiction writer who coined the term 'cyberspace'. I live an active life in an inner suburb of London with a number of travel modes at my disposal. This allows me to conclude that a future of liveable cities is indeed attainable without the car as central to urban life.

Sources, Further Reading and References

Selected published sources are shown below for each chapter, with details in the *References* section. Websites are not generally cited exactly since specific addresses often change or are discontinued over time. However, extant web sources can usually be found by searching a few key words from the text, for example 'Seattle traffic' finds the website for real time traffic conditions in the Seattle area mentioned in Chapter 5.

The main statistical source employed is the ***National Travel Survey*** (NTS), an annual survey of the travel behaviour of some 20,000 residents of Great Britain, commissioned each year by the Department for Transport (DfT). Another DfT source is ***Transport Statistics Great Britain***. For London, the annual series *Travel in London*, published by Transport for London, is invaluable. International statistics are compiled by the International Transport Forum of the OECD.

The central argument in this book has been developed in a series of papers published in peer-reviewed journals. The key papers included in the *References* section are Metz (2008a), Metz (2010), Metz (2012) and Metz (2013a). My earlier book, *The Limits to Travel,* provides a broader context for the present rather concise account (Metz 2008b). My current website www.davidmetz.org includes background material. I will comment there on matters following publication of the present book.

Introduction

Phil Goodwin's articles introducing the idea of 'peak car' were published in *Local Transport Today* in 2010-11 and summarised in Goodwin (2012a,b]. He and Gordon Stokes edited a special issue of the journal *Transport Reviews*, bringing together a number of timely papers (Volume 33(3), 2013), with an overview (Goodwin and Van Dender, 2013).

Chapter 1: Three Eras of Travel

Evolutionary origins of human mobility: Metz (2008b); recent findings are described by Dobbs (2013). Sahlins (1974) and Kelly (1995) report behaviour in surviving hunter-gatherer societies.

History of transport: Wolmar (2007) for railways in Britain; Lay (1992) for the world's roads and the vehicles that use them.

General development of travel in Britain and elsewhere over the past forty years: Metz (2008a, 2008b, 2010, 2012, 2013a, 2013b). Seminal papers on the constancy of travel time are Marchetti (1994) and Schafer and Victor (2000).

Cessation of growth of car travel: Puentes and Tomer (2008), Millard-Ball and Schipper (2011), Goodwin (2012a,b), Le Vine and Jones (2012), Kuhnimhof et al (2012), Puentes (2012); Gargett (2012); Dutzik and Baxandall (2013); *Transport Reviews* 33(3) 2013.

Chapter 2: City Living

History of city transport: Crafts and Leunig (2005); Pooley et al (2006). Transport in London in the nineteenth century: White (2007). The relationship between cities and transport is discussed by Hall (1994) and Newman and Kenworthy (2007).

Population data for London: 2011 Census and Greater London Authority projections. Car use and other travel data for London: *Travel in London Report 5* issued by Transport for London. Car use in other cities: Newman and

Kenworthy (2011), Metz (2013a). Relation between demographic change and travel behaviour: Metz (2012) and Metz (2013a).

Younger people driving less: Puentes (2012), Kuhnimhof et al (2012), Le Vine and Jones (2012), Stokes (2013).

Public transport in Europe: Buehler and Pucher (2012). Grescoe (2012) writes attractively about public transport in major cities. Begg (2013) provides a comprehensive analysis of London's transport system.

IBM regularly monitors traffic congestion in major cities in its Commuter Pain Survey. Keith Gessen wrote about Moscow traffic in the New Yorker of 2 August 2010.

Key books on current perceptions of cities are Florida (2005) and Glaeser (2011). The case for urban renaissance in Britain: Rogers (2005).

Chapter 3: Suburban Societies

Population location in relation to transport: Headicar (2009). Demographic factors influencing travel demand: Metz (2012). Transition to adult life: Billari and Liefbroer (2010). Disability in later life: Vaupel (2010).

UK population projections are those of the Office of National Statistics issued in March 2012 (based on the 2010 population estimate), plus some subsequent higher projections that reflect the outcome of the 2011 Census. Global population projections are the most recent from UN Department of Social and Economic Affairs, Population Division.

Cairns et al (2008) reviewed the evidence on 'smarter choices'.

The case for buses in suburbia has been persuasively set out by Mees (2010). The UK Competition Commission reported on local buses outside London in 2011. Factors that promote bus use: White (2008). Public transport in Hong Kong: Lo et al (2008). Concessionary bus fares: Dargay, Liu and Toner (2010). ITNAmerica supports community-based auto transport systems for seniors.

Teleactivities: Andreev, Salomon and Pliskina (2010). Online retailing: Cullinane (2009). British households' use of online shopping: National Travel Survey. US data on online retailing from Forrester Research.

Chapter 4: Going Global

Migration: Moses (2006); Stalker (2008); Goldin, Cameron and Balarajan (2011); Black et al (2011). Polish migration to the UK: 2011 Census.

Travel to and from the UK: data from the International Passenger Survey of the Office of National Statistics. Passengers using UK airports: Civil Aviation Authority data. Information on UK residents not flying from the National Travel Survey.

The Airports Commission is publishing in 2013 a series of papers on demand for air travel and supply of airport facilities in the UK.

Chapter 5: Speed Limits

Car energy use: MacKay (2008). Battery technology: Service (2011). Oil supplies: Murray and King (2012).

Benefits from road improvements: 'Highways Agency (2011), Post Opening Project Evaluation of Major Schemes (2002 to 2009)'.

Road freight transport: McKinnon (2010).

Road pricing and 'predictive navigation': Metz (2008c). Public attitudes and responses to congestion from Department for Transport surveys.

Road tunnels are discussed in the 2013 Report of the Roads Task Force established by the Mayor of London and in the response of Transport for London. The technical notes and international case studies prepared by TfL to inform this study are valuable source on urban road management practice.

Genetics and mobility: Jones (2000): Nalls et al (2009).

Bicycle use in Britain: Goodwin (2013); in North America: Pucher, Buehler and Sienem (2011). Parkinson's disease and cycling: Aerts, Adbo and Bloem (2011). Transport for London issued an Analysis of Cycling Potential in 2010.

Disruptive innovation: Christensen (1997). An optimistic view of driverless cars: Burns (2013); a current perspective from Burkhard Bilger in the New Yorker of 25 November 2013.

Chapter 6: Decisions, Decisions

The conventional approach to transport cost-benefit appraisal is set out in the Department for Transport's Transport Analysis Guidance: WebTAG. Recent reviews supporting current practice: Worsley (2011), Mackie and Worsley (2013). My critique of this methodology: Metz (2008a).

The Department for Transport website has extensive material on High Speed 2, the most recently published in October 2013. The National Audit Office issued a report on HS2 in May 2013. For sceptical discussions: of the regional benefits, Tomaney and Marques (2013); of value for money, New Economics Foundation, *High Speed 2: The best we can do?* (June 2013); and of 'megaprojects' generally, Flyvjberg (2009). The House of Commons Public Accounts Committee issued a report on HS1 in 2012.

A website is available for the Nine Elms development. The Financial Times of 10 December 2012 reported the financial arrangements for the Tube extension. The same newspaper reported the move of company head offices to London on 17 February 2010.

The Department for Transport issued a policy paper, *Action for Roads*, in July 2013, summarising investment plans. This was accompanied by *Road Transport Forecasts 2013.* BMW's research establishment, the Institute for Mobility Research, issued a report in 2013: 'Mobility Y'the Emerging Travel Patterns of Generation Y.

Chapter 7: Travellers' Tales

History of travel writing: Whitfield (2011). Classic era of British travel writing: Fussell (1980).

Human universals and mental modules: Brown (1991); Pinker (2002); Tooby and Cosmides (2005).

Evolutionary basis for narrative: Sugiyama (2001), Gottschall (2013).

Chapter 8: Fourth Era Travel

Technological development slowing: Cowen (2011), Gordon (2012).

Demand saturation: Metz (2013). Low growth economy: Jackson (2009).

Green metropolis: Owen (2009); Dodman (2009); Glaeser (2011).

Future global vehicle numbers: Sperling and Gordon (2009). Alternative forms of car ownership: Cairns and Harmer (2011). Car parking: Bates and Liebling (2012).

Features of Fourth Era travel: Metz (2013).

References

Aerts, M., Adbo, W. and Bloem, B. (2011) The "bicycle sign" for atypical parkinsonism, *The Lancet*, 377, 125-126.

Andreev, P., Salomon, I. and Pliskina, N. (2010) Review: State of Teleactivities, *Transportation Research Part C*, 18(1), 3-20.

Bates, J. and Liebling, D. (2012) *Spaced Out: Perspectives on Parking Policy*, London: RAC Foundation.

Begg, D. (2013) *World Class? London's Transport: Progress and Future Challenges*, London: Siemens.

Billari, F. and Liefbroer, A. (2010) Towards a New Pattern of Transition to Adulthood? *Advances in Life Course Research*, 15(2-3), 59-75.

Black, R., Bennett, R., Thomas, S. and Beddington, J. (2011) Climate Change: Migration as Adaptation, *Nature* 478, 447-449.

Brown, D. (1991) *Human Universals*, New York: McGraw-Hill.

Buehler, R. and Pucher, J. (2012) Demand for Public Transport in Germany and the USA: an Analysis of Rider Characteristics, *Transport Reviews*, 32(5), 541-567.

Burns, L. (2013) Sustainable Mobility: a Vision of our Transport Future, *Nature* 497, 181-182.

Cairns, S. and Harmer, S. (2011) *Accessing Cars: Insights from International Experience*, London: RAC Foundation.

Cairns, S., Sloman, L, Newson, C., Anable, J., Kirkbride, A. and Goodwin, P. (2008) Smarter Choices: assessing the potential to achieve traffic reduction using 'soft measures', *Transport Reviews*, 28(5), 593-618.

Christensen, C. (1997) *The Innovator's Dilemma: When New Technologies Cause Great Firms to Fail*, Boston: Harvard University Press.

Cowen, T. (2011) *The Great Stagnation*, New York: Dutton.

Crafts, N. and Leunig, T. (2005) *The historical significance of transport for economic growth and productivity: background paper for the Eddington Report*; Research Annexes volume 1, Department for Transport, London.

Cullinane, S. (2009) From Bricks to Clicks: the Impact of Online Retailing on Transport and the Environment, *Transport Reviews*, 29(6), 759-776.

Dargay, J., Liu, R. and Toner, J. (2010) Concessionary Bus Fares in England: the Impact on Bus Travel by the Over-60s. European Transport Conference paper.

Dobbs, D. (2013) Restless Genes, *National Geographic*, January issue.

Dodman, D. (2009) Blaming cities for climate change? An analysis of urban greenhouse gas emissions inventories, *Environment and Urbanization*, 21(1), 185-201.

Dutzik, T. and Baxandall, P. (2013) *A New Direction: Our Changing Relationship with Driving and the Implications for America's Future,* Boston MA: US PIRG Education Fund.

Florida, R. (2005) *Cities and the Creative Class,* Abingdon: Routledge.

Flyvbjerg, B. (2009) Survival of the Unfitest: why the worst infrastructure gets built—and what we can do about it. *Oxford Review of Economic Policy,* 25(3), 344-367.

Fussell, P. (1980) *Abroad: British Literary Traveling between the Wars,* Oxford: Oxford University Press.

Gargett , D. (2012) *Traffic Growth: Modelling a Global Phenomenon,* Report 128, Canberra: Bureau of Infrastructure, Transport and Regional Economics (BITRE).

Glaeser, E. (2011) *Triumph of the City,* London: Macmillan.

Goldin, I., Cameron, G. and Balarajan, M. (2011) *Exceptional People: how migration shaped our world and will define our future,* Princeton NJ: Princeton University Press.

Goodwin, P. (2012a) Three Views on Peak Car, *World Transport Policy and Practice,* 17.4, 8-17.

Goodwin, P. (2012b) *Peak Travel, Peak Car and the Future of Mobility: Evidence, Unresolved Issues, Policy Implications, and a Research Agenda,* Discussion Paper 2012-13, International Transport Forum, Paris: OECD.

Goodwin, P. (2013) *Get Britain Cycling: Report from the Inquiry,* London: All-Party Parliamentary Cycling Group.

Goodwin, P. and Van Dender, K. (2013) 'Peak Car' – Themes and Issues, *Transport Reviews,* 33(3), 243-254.

Gordon, R. (2012) *Is US Economic Growth Over? Faltering Innovation Confronts the Six Headwinds.* Policy Insight No. 63, London: Centre for Economic Policy Research.

Gottschall, J. (2013) The Storytelling Animal, New York: Mariner Books, Houghton Mifflin Harcourt.

Hall, P. (1994) Squaring the circle: can we resolve the Clarkian paradox?, *Environment and Planning B: Planning and Design*, 21, S79-S94.

Headicar, P. (2009) *Transport Policy and Planning in Great Britain*, Abingdon: Routledge.

Jackson, T. (2009) *Prosperity Without Growth: the Transition to a Sustainable Economy*, London: Sustainable Development Commission.

Jones, S. (2000) *The Language of the Genes (revised edition)*, London: Flamingo.

Kelly, R. (1995) *The Foraging Spectrum: diversity in hunter-gatherers' lifeways*, Washington: Smithsonian Institution Press.

Kuhnimhof, T., Armoogum, J., Buehler, R., Dargay, J., Denstali, J. and Yamamoto, T. (2012) Men shape a downward trend in car use amongst young adults – evidence from six industrialised countries. *Transport Reviews* 32(6), pp. 761-779.

Lay, M. (1992) *Ways of the World: a History of the World's Roads and the Vehicles That Used Them*, New Brunswick, NJ: Rutgers University Press.

Le Vine, S. and Jones, P. (2012) *On the Move: making sense of car and train travel trends in Britain*, London: RAC Foundation.

Lo, K., Tang, S. and Wang, D. (2008) Managing the Accessibility on Mass Public Transit: the Case of Hong Kong, *Journal of Transport and Land Use*, 1(2), 23-49.

MacKay, D. (2008) *Sustainable Energy - without the hot air. Section III A*, http://www.inference.phy.cam.ac.uk/withouthotair/

Mackie, P. and Worsley, T. (2013) International Comparisons of Transport Appraisal Practice: Overview Report, Leeds: Institute for Transport Studies.

Marchetti, C. (1994) Anthropological invariants in travel behaviour, *Technological Forecasting and Social Change*, 47(1), 75-88.

McKinnon, A. (2010) *Transport Challenges and Opportunities: Briefing Paper on the Freight Transport Sector*, London: Commission for Integrated Transport.

Mees, P. (2010) *Transport for Suburbia*, London: Earthscan.

Metz, D. (2008a) The Myth of Travel Times Saving, *Transport Reviews*, 28(3), 321-336.

Metz, D. (2008b) *The Limits to Travel*, London: Earthscan/Routledge.

Metz, D. (2008c) National Road Pricing: a Critique and an Alternative, *Proceedings of the Institution of Civil Engineers Transport*, 161 (TR3), 161-174.

Metz, D. (2010) Saturation of Demand for Daily Travel, *Transport Reviews*, 30(5), 659-674.

Metz, D. (2012) Demographic Determinants of Daily Travel Demand, *Transport Policy*, 21(1) 20-25.

Metz, D. (2013a) Peak Car and Beyond: the Fourth Era of Travel, *Transport Reviews*, 33(3), 255-270.

Metz, D. (2013b) Mobility, Access and Choice: a New Source of Evidence, *Journal of Transport and Land Use*, 6(2), 1-4.

Millard-Ball, A. and Schipper, L. (2011) Are we reaching peak travel? Trends in passenger transport in eight industrialized countries, *Transport Reviews*, 31(3), 357-378.

Moses, J. (2006) *International Migration*, London: Zed Books, London.

Murray, J. and King, D. (2012) Climate Policy; Oil's Tipping Point Has Passed. *Nature*, 481, 433-435.

Nalls M., Simon-Sanchez, J., Gibbs, J., Paisan-Ruiz, C., Bras, J., et al. (2009) Measures of Autozygosity in Decline: Globalization, Urbanization, and Its Implications for Medical Genetics. *PLoS Genet*, 5(3), e1000415.

Newman, P. and Kenworthy. J. (2007) *Greening urban transportation,* in State of the World 2007: Our Urban Future, Worldwatch Institute, London: Earthscan.

Newman, P. and Kenworthy. J. (2011) Peak Car Use: Understanding the Demise of Automobile Dependence, *World Transport Policy and Practice,* 17(2), 31-42.

Owen, D. (2009) *Green Metropolis,* New York: Riverhead Books.

Pooley, C., Turnbull, J. and Adams, M. (2006) The impact of new transport technologies on intraurban mobility: a view from the past, *Environment and Planning Part A,* 38(2), 253 – 267.

Pucher, J., Buehler, R. and Seinem, M. (2011) Bicycling Renaissance in North America, Transportation Research Part A, 45(6), 451-475.

Pinker, S. (2002) *The Blank Slate,* London: Allen Lane.

Puentes, R. and Tomer, A. (2008) *The road less travelled: an analysis of vehicle miles travelled trends in the U.S.* Washington: The Brookings Institution.

Puentes, R. (2012) *Have Americans Hit Peak Travel? A Discussion of the Changes in US Driving Habits,* Discussion Paper 2012-14, International Transport Forum, Paris: OECD.

Rogers, R. (2005) *Towards a Strong Urban Renaissance,* London: Urban Task Force.

Sahlins, M. (1974) *Stone Age Economics,* London: Tavistock Publications.

Schafer, A. and Victor, D. (2000) The future mobility of the world population, *Transportation Research Part A,* 34(3), 171 -205.

Service, R. (2011) Getting There, *Science,* 332, 1494-1496.

Sperling, D. and Gordon, D. (2009) *Two Billion Cars,* New York: Oxford University Press.

Stalker, P. (2008) *The No-Nonsense Guide to International Migration*, Oxford: New Internationalist Publications.

Stokes, G. (2013) The Prospects for Future Levels of Car Access and Use, *Transport Reviews*, 33(3), 360-373.

Sugiyama, M. (2001) Narrative Theory and Function: Why Evolution Matters, *Philosophy and Literature*, 25(20), 233-250.

Tomaney, J. and Marques, P. (2013) Evidence, Policy and the Politics of Regional Development: the Case for High Speed Rail in the United Kingdom, Environment and Planning Part C , 31(3), 414-427.

Tooby, J. and Cosmides, L. (2005) *Conceptual Foundations of Evolutionary Psychology*, in Buss, D. (ed) *The Handbook of Evolutionary Psychology*, Hoboken NJ: Whiley.

Vaupel, J. (2010) Biodemography of human ageing, *Nature*, 464, pp. 536-542.

White, J. (2007) *London in the Nineteenth Century*, London: Jonathan Cape.

White, P. (2008) *Factors Affecting the Decline of Bus Use in the Metropolitan Areas*, University of Westminster.

Whitfield, P. (2011) *Travel: a literary history*, Oxford: Bodleian Library.

Wolmar, C. (2007) *Fire and Steam: a New History of the Railways in Britain*, London: Atlantic Books.

Worsley, T. (2011) *The evolution of London's Crossrail Scheme and the development of the Department for Transport's economic appraisal methods.* Discussion Paper 2011-27, International Transport Forum, Paris: OECD.

Acknowledgements

I am grateful to colleagues at the Centre for Transport Studies, University College London, for their hospitality while this book was being written. I have benefited from discussions held in London under the auspices of the Transport Statistics Users Group, the Transport Economists Group, the Transport Planning Society, as well as at UCL seminars. I am obliged to a number of colleagues and friends who have kindly read and commented on the manuscript: Alise Kirtley, Sebastian Balfour, David Caplin, Mary Clemmey, Peter Jones, Simon Lister, Sebastian Loew, Ben Metz, Kit Mitchell, Donald Sassoon, Peter Stonham and Alan Wenban-Smith.

Index